REAL CANADIAN PIRATES

Buccaneers & Rogues of the North

Geordie Telfer

FOLK LORE PUBLISHING

The Publisher: Folklore Publishing
Website: www.folklorepublishing.com

Library and Archives Canada Cataloguing in Publication

Telfer, Geordie
    Real Canadian Pirates / Geordie Telfer

ISBN 13: 978-1-894864-70-1
ISBN 10: 1-894864-70-0

    1. Pirates—Canada—Biography. I. Title.

HV6805.T45 2007   64.16′4092271   C2007-902116-6

Project Director: Faye Boer
Project Editor: Kathy van Denderen
Cover Image: Illustration by Howard Pyle. Illustration used courtesy of The Granger Collection, New York.

We acknowledge the support of the Alberta Foundation for the Arts for our publishing program.

We acknowledge the financial support of the Government of Canada through the Book Publishing Industry Development Program (BPIDP) for our publishing activities.

Canada Council
for the Arts

Conseil des Arts
du Canada

Canadian
Heritage

Patrimoine
canadien

PC:P5

Contents

Dedication

This book is happily and proudly dedicated to
my parents, Rose & Keith.

Acknowledgements

For their generosity and help, my thanks go to
Jim Eagan,
arguably the leading authority on Bill Johnston,
and
Carolyn McTaggart, inarguably the leading
authority on Gunpowder Gertie.

Introduction

Shiver me timbers, eh?

CANADIANS ARE FASCINATED BY OTHER CANADIANS, especially other Canadians who are famous, noteworthy or—pirates. If it were left to pop culture to paint a picture of a Canadian pirate, we might see a figure wearing a toque with a skull and crossbones on it, brandishing a cutlass in one hand, a hockey stick in the other and guzzling gallons of rum and maple syrup (or politely inventing a donut flavour combining the two). Of course the reality is far different.

Like much of Canada's history, the story of piracy in Canada starts with Europeans coming here in search of new opportunities. Admittedly, they came in search of new opportunities to raid, steal and plunder but, come to think of it, that's what brought Europeans here in the first place; these days we politely call the ones who weren't pirates, "explorers."

And, again like much of Canadian history, the middle section of the story quickly shifts gears to revolve around tense relations with our neighbours to the south, known to the world at large as "Americans." It would be a mistake to suggest that Canadian pirates were somehow patriots—in fact, most of them were aggressive opportunists who wanted to make money—but the looming presence below the 49th parallel is a constant presence in the middle third of this book.

Within these pages you'll read about plenty of larger-than-life characters who, like the country itself are big, unruly and sometimes (but not often) conflicted from within. Of course all of these people were pirates first and foremost—only rarely does nationalism play a part. For the most part, the outlaws you're about to meet just wanted to acquire riches by whatever means possible, though some of them were better at it than others.

Since pirates didn't keep diaries, in the early chapters of this book, situations and actions have been reconstructed as closely as possible from the information available. In later chapters, details have been drawn from courtroom transcripts and trial notes. Anywhere that dialogue appears in quotation marks, these are the words of the perpetrators, and their victims as recounted by eyewitnesses.

For unfamiliar terms, see the Glossary at the back of this book.

Beyond that, smooth sailing and happy reading to you.

Geordie Telfer
Toronto
March 2007

CHAPTER ONE

Peter Easton
(The Pirate Admiral)

Happiness lies only in that which excites, and the only thing that excites is crime.

—Marquis de Sade

TODAY, HARBOUR GRACE, NEWFOUNDLAND, IS A QUIET town with a population of about 3000. Like many maritime towns, its local economy is centred around catching and processing fish. There are plants and facilities for just about every step on a fish's journey from seabed to dinner plate. Harbour Grace is also building its tourist industry, and since most visitors are interested more in sightseeing than fish-gutting, the town offers an engaging menu of attractions: a regatta, an annual dog show (sponsored by the Conception Bay Kennel Club), the Trinity-Conception Fall Fair and, for those with an eye to beauty, the Miss Newfoundland and Labrador Pageant. All in all a pleasant, if typical-sounding, east coast community.

But 400 years ago, Harbour Grace was anything but typical. It was home to cannon fire, high adventure and vast hoards of plundered treasure. It saw raging battles, surprise invasions and triumphant homecomings. From its vantage point on the west shore of Conception Bay, Harbour Grace served with distinction as the stronghold and home base for one of the most successful pirates in history— the so-called pirate admiral Peter Easton.

HARBOUR GRACE, NEWFOUNDLAND (CIRCA 1612)

Peter Easton looked keenly at the approaching shore as his flagship, the *Happy Adventure*, sliced through the waters of the North Atlantic. With three masts, square-rigged sails and double decks, the *Happy Adventure* was an impressive sight. Standing on the upper deck, her captain was a figure of authority and command. He was a strongly built man with dark hair and the tanned skin of a sailor. His clothes were cut for the rough-and-tumble life at sea, but they were also well made, for Captain Easton was no scurvy sea dog: He was a gentleman of means from an old family. He also happened to be at the pinnacle of his career as a pirate.

On this day, Easton was leading his pirate fleet back to the beckoning shores of their coastal haven at Harbour Grace, "New-Found-Land." The ships' timbers were creaking under the shared weight of a huge treasure haul, seized during a daring raid on the Spanish colony of Puerto Rico. There, Easton's forces had set their sights on El Morro Castle, a famous Spanish citadel that had previously withstood an attack by the intrepid explorer and sometime pirate, Sir Francis Drake. But where Drake had failed, Easton prevailed.

When the sails of Easton's ships appeared on the horizon, the Spanish were completely unprepared, and Easton's pirate army easily overpowered the castle's defences. Soon, his men were filling the holds of their ships with ingots of gold and silver smelted from the local mines. They also plundered vast hoards of Incan, Mayan and Aztec art treasures wrought from precious metals and encrusted in shining jewels. To add insult to injury, Easton also captured a Spanish ship, the *San Sebastien*, that had already been conveniently loaded with treasure to take back to Spain.

As the pirate armada came within sight of Harbour Grace, Easton was anticipating a triumphant return to friendly shores—but this time something was amiss.

He could see that between his treasure-laden fleet and the mouth of the harbour, there was a dotted line of lightly coloured sails heading his way. This was not good. Easton enjoyed a friendly arrangement with merchants in the area: He acted as an informal enforcer, protecting local stores of fish and salt from would-be raiders. In return, such authorities as there were turned a blind eye to his pirating and gave him safe haven, free from troublesome legal interference by the Crown. The sudden appearance of so many ships, now sailing out to meet him, could only mean one thing—

some rival force had arrived in his absence and moved in on his turf.

He was right.

While Easton had been so profitably employed, stealing from the Spanish, a fleet of French Basques had sailed into Harbour Grace and taken over the town, including the fort that Easton's pirates called home. And now, the rival Basques, led by a ship called the *St. Malo,* were sailing out to engage the home team. Easton, with 11 ships full of fabulous wealth, was even more motivated than usual to come out on top—and what happened next only increased his reputation as a man who was invincible.

Peter Easton, the pirate admiral, completely destroyed the invading fleet, either sinking or capturing every last one of the doomed Basque vessels. The *St. Malo* finished her days run aground on a small islet near the mouth of the harbour. Little more than a speck of rock in the ocean, the area was later christened Easton's Islet, then bastardized into Eastern Isle and appears today as Eastern Rock.

After they wiped out the rival fleet at sea, Easton's forces went ashore and drove out the invaders, recapturing their fort and retaking the town. Forty-seven of Easton's men were killed and subsequently buried at nearby Bear Cove, an area known to this day as the Pirates' Graveyard.

Finally, perhaps needing to blow off a bit of steam, Easton's men unloaded the treasure from the *San Sebastien*, stripped her of sail, rope and armament, then burnt the Spanish ship down to the waterline.

It was 1602 when Peter Easton first arrived in Newfoundland. He came then not as a pirate, but rather a *privateer*, under the good graces of Queen Elizabeth I of England. Privateers were essentially pirates licensed by the Crown to plunder, pillage and otherwise harass the shipping routes of enemy nations. In the early 1600s Elizabethan England was locked in a knock-down, winner-take-all naval war with Spain, and the fledgling English navy was far from being the mighty weapon it would one day become. So, to gain every possible advantage, Queen Elizabeth (like many a monarch before and after) started issuing "letters of marque" to private citizens wealthy enough to outfit their own ships.

Letters of marque set out terms whereby privateers could board and capture ships of enemy nations, seize the cargo and sell it at a profit. In theory, the privateers were supposed to split the proceeds with the Crown, but this didn't always happen. However, kings and queens were happy to overlook the occasional lapse in profit-sharing because of the incredible economic damage privateers wrought on the fortunes of enemy nations.

Privateers also guarded the convoys that ferried boatloads of precious goods back and forth between the New World and Europe. It was in this capacity that Easton first arrived in Newfoundland, and it was here that his legend began. Entrusted with guarding England's fishing fleet, Easton seems to have found time for an early extracurricular adventure when he freed a beautiful Irish maiden, named Sheila O'Connor, from the clutches of a crew of Dutch privateers. Known ever after as Sheila "Nagira" (from old Gaelic slang for "beautiful"), this comely lass subsequently married Gilbert Pike, one of Easton's lieutenants, and the two of them begat the line of Pikes whose descendants still bear their name throughout Newfoundland.

When Queen Elizabeth died in 1603, her successor, James I, began his reign by making peace with Spain. This meant that English privateers were suddenly deprived of an enemy whose riches they were entitled to rob. Accordingly, many of them turned to outright piracy. Back in England, Peter Easton threw in his lot with a prominent family of troublemakers, the Killigrews, also known as the Robber Barons of Land's End. The Killigrews were a colourful bunch; well connected to royalty, the entire clan lived on the edge of the law, seemingly free from meaningful prosecution. One of them even tried to sell England to the Spanish for 10,000 gold crowns, though how he planned to smuggle an entire country out of itself remains unclear.

From their ancestral stronghold, Castle Pendennis in Cornwall, the Killigrews acted as financial backers for local pirates, helping to sell the captured booty and then taking a substantial cut of the profits. They also controlled miles and miles of inland waterways behind their castle, giving fugitive pirate ships a safe place to hide from the English navy. But like any thriving business venture, the Killigrews soon found that healthy growth brought with it the need to delegate. Fully occupied with their many crooked intrigues on land and in the corridors of power, they needed someone to manage their interests at sea.

And that was how, in 1610, Peter Easton found himself recognized as the *de facto* leader of about 40 ships that patrolled the English Channel in a highly organized but completely illegal fashion. Honest merchants shipping their wares through ports, like Bristol and Pool, had to pay protection money to Easton in order to avoid damage to their vessels. The system seems to have worked quite well, with Easton wielding a fearsome enough reputation that few, if any, merchant ships ever tried to resist. Most ships' masters were so anxious to avoid conflict that they would willingly hand over provisions, and even crew members, so long as their main cargo remained untouched.

Unfortunately, as the saying goes, all good things must end—including rampant thievery on the high seas. Eventually, a group of merchants from the port city of Bristol petitioned the Crown for protection from predators like Easton. Soon, Easton learned that a high-spirited 23-year-old named Henry Mainwarring (probably pronounced "Mannering") had been commissioned to bring him in.

Mainwarring was a gentleman sailor; he seems to have come from a background several rungs higher on the social ladder than even Easton's. Something of a renaissance man, Mainwarring was by turns a soldier, a scholar, a sailor, a politician and a lawyer. He also appears to have been quite wealthy, for when he discovered that the navy wanted to give him rotten, worm-eaten ships to hunt down Easton, he mustered his own fleet and outfitted it with help from his friends.

Meanwhile, Easton had caught wind of Mainwarring's preparations and was considering his options. He could engage Mainwarring in battle with every expectation of victory. But since Mainwarring was technically a representative of the King, giving battle in British waters could be interpreted as an attack on England itself. Daring, but not stupid, Easton knew that even he could not afford to have the King of England on his bad side. On the whole, running away seemed to be the most prudent thing to do. That way, if Mainwarring followed him, Easton could safely give battle and, being clear of English waters, could not be accused of making war on the King. If Mainwarring did not give chase, then Easton could happily move on to new waters.

During a short cruise down the coast of Africa, Easton thought about his next steps. He needed to find somewhere that he could set up camp—a location free from rival pirates and well away from the English navy. But where? His thoughts turned back to his days as a privateer...

St. John's, Newfoundland (Summer 1611)

Richard Whitbourne had been many things in his life. He had worked his way up from ship's mate to the Fishing Admiral of the Port of St. John's, a post that made him one of the most powerful men in Newfoundland. But one thing he had no intention of becoming was a pirate, though that was precisely what this Peter Easton fellow seemed to be suggesting.

Nearly four months previous, Easton and his 10 ships had sailed into the harbour and dropped anchor. In Whitbourne's own words, the ships were "well furnished and very rich." During that time, Captain Whitbourne had been wined and dined nearly every day in the posh captain's cabin at the stern of the *Happy Adventure*. At first, the excellent meals, succulent sweetmeats and rare vintages had been quite enjoyable. But now, after 11 solid weeks of being plied with rich foods that tightened his britches, and fruity wines that loosened his judgment, the novelty was beginning to wear off. And behind it all was the constant torrent of talking from this man Easton, the pleas and promises issuing forth from his lips in a veritable river of words that went something like this:

Would Captain Whitbourne supply Captain Easton with local fishermen to serve as crew on his (Captain Easton's) ships?

No, Captain Whitbourne would not.

Would Captain Whitbourne give (not sell, but give) Captain Easton provisions, weapons and munitions for his ships?

No, he would not.

Did Captain Whitbourne realize that, when Captain Easton had been a royally sanctioned privateer in these waters in 1602, he had been legally entitled to (and often did) requisition supplies and arms from official government stores?

Yes, Captain Whitbourne most assuredly did realize this. However, did Captain Easton realize that he (Captain Easton) was in fact no longer a privateer and as such was regrettably no longer entitled to material assistance from the Crown?

Captain Easton did realize this. However, did Captain Whitbourne realize that if he helped Captain Easton, he (Captain Whitbourne) would certainly be handsomely rewarded?

Was Captain Easton aware of the fact that Captain Whitbourne held a vice admiralty commission making it his (Captain Whitbourne's) sworn duty to fight piracy?

Would Captain Whitbourne like another glass of wine?

And it went on like this for days and days and days—nearly 120 of them. It was like playing chess with an equally matched opponent who refused to give up. On the one hand there was Whitbourne, who didn't want to offend Easton because his fleet of 10 ships boasted far more armament and fire-power than all the ships in St. John's. On the other hand was Easton, looking for a relatively permanent base for his ships and men, so he needed to maintain the goodwill of the British authorities governing Newfoundland.

At last, after a long summer of attempted, but unsuccessful bribery, Easton realized that Whitbourne would not be corrupted, and he gave up (one also suspects his ship-board wine cellar was becoming depleted). Whitbourne went ashore with considerable relief, later writing that "I was kept eleven weeks under his command, and had from him many golden promises and much wealth offered to be put into my hands." For his part, Easton weighed anchor and set off to look for easier sailing, knowing that he probably wouldn't have to go far.

The pirate admiral's fleet had come west across the Atlantic with skeleton crews in her ships; that is, just enough men to sail them. Calm and majestic as they seem to us today, the ships that pirates sailed in were actually complex machines that needed specially trained crews to operate them. Easton's flagship, the *Happy Adventure*, for example, weighed about 350 tons and would have carried from six to nine separate sails that had to be raised, lowered

and trimmed almost *simultaneously*. Then they had
to be secured (or "made fast") with a complex
arrangement of pulleys and ropes, which in turn
had to be fastened with specific knots in a specific
order, often done in no more than a few seconds.

The ship also would have carried an extra "lateen"
sail at the stern that made her more agile and able
to execute sharp turns (or "come about") very
quickly, as the wind caught the stern of the boat.
For armament she would have carried a full com-
plement of 30–40 full-sized cannons in addition to
numerous, small swivel guns. Also, the iconic-
spoked steering wheel, familiar to us through movies and illustrations, had not been invented yet.
Instead, the rudder was turned by yet more ropes
that required yet more men to operate it.

A ship engaged in some lawful enterprise like
fishing or shipping might require 30–40 men, but
Easton liked to crew his ships with 180 men *each*—
and with good reason. Pirate crews had to be large
so that there were always enough men on hand to
pilot the ship as their crew mates boarded and captured the ships they preyed on. Extra men were
also needed to hold unwilling crews prisoner, off-
load cargo and possibly stay on the prize and sail it
as a new addition to the pirate fleet. That meant
that with 10 ships, Easton needed about 1800 men.

After his lack of success with Richard Whitbourne in St. John's, Easton decided to look for
smaller settlements where he could simply take

whatever, or whoever, he wanted. At the back of his mind may have lurked the notion that life was hard in the more remote outposts and that he might find more men willing to chase the winds of fortune under a pirate's flag. Indeed, in modern-day Newfoundland it is fashionable to think of Easton as a sort of liberator, giving the wretched fishmongers of the east coast a chance at something better. In reality, it is doubtful that he held such noble ideals—Easton wanted money, needed men and didn't care whether they came willingly or by force. Furthermore, he had no qualms about enslaving unwilling fishermen to do his bidding.

Over the next few months his ships prowled the coastal waters, landing at smaller colonies such as those at Cape Race and Cupid. From places like these he took more than 1500 men; some of them went willingly, but most were forced into service. He also captured more than 100 guns and cannons from different English ships and installed them on his own.

Now armed to the teeth, well provisioned and boasting an army that was at least large, if not willing, Easton set up base in Harbour Grace. From there, he proceeded to capture ships of all nationalities without prejudice or preference. In subsequent battles he captured 25 French ships, 12 Portuguese ships and one Flemish vessel thrown in for good measure. In all cases he gained not only the ships themselves but also their valuable cargoes.

Paradoxically, he also became a protector to the same outposts he had robbed of men and guns. During the winters, when fishing colonies operated with skeleton staffs, their supplies were particularly vulnerable to pirates like Easton himself. And so, in at least one instance, ships from the colony at Cupid docked at Harbour Grace and willingly unloaded 15 tons of valuable preserving salt into the hands of Easton and his men. For a fee, the pirates would guard the salt over the winter until the colonists came back to reclaim it in the spring. Whether this cozy arrangement worked as well in practice as it did in theory remains unknown. Such a huge quantity of salt was valuable enough that Easton could have profitably sold it to a different fishing colony or even ransomed it back to the colony from whence it came.

With the money rolling in from his many conquests (and possibly a bit on the side from illicit salt sales), Easton proceeded to set himself up in style. While the pirate crews—who were decidedly not gentlemen—lived in a sort of fortified compound, their captain wanted something better, and so he built a large house on Fox Hill in the nearby settlement of Ferryland.

Fox Hill was the perfect location for a busy pirate: It was close to major ocean shipping routes; guarding the mouth of the harbour was a wooded island that was an ideal vantage point for sentinels on the lookout for invading ships; there was a small natural harbour where ships could be repaired;

and rising over the beach was a hill that commanded a strategic view in all directions. From Fox Hill and Harbour Grace, Easton mounted many expeditions at great profit, including the raid on Puerto Rico in which he captured the *San Sebastien*.

For the most part, Easton concentrated on attacking England's old enemy, Spain. He focused almost all of his piratical activities on depriving Spanish treasure ships of their spoils. His sails were a constant presence in their shipping lanes, lurking just over the horizon, waiting to strike. This was likely not due to any lingering patriotism on his part, but more to the fact that the Spaniards, with their Central and South American colonies, simply had the best treasure.

However, Easton wasn't above taking the odd English prize as well, once capturing a Cornwall-owned slave ship bound for the Spanish colonies. When he brought the captured ship back to Newfoundland, Richard Whitbourne seems to have been alarmed that, slaves or no slaves, Easton had attacked an English ship. He managed to persuade Easton to return the ship to her rightful owner, and off it went, back across the Atlantic to England.

At this point the pirate admiral realized that over the course of his illustrious if highly illegal career, he had done much to cause the King of England to find displeasure with him. Should he ever want to leave the Newfoundland shores for more civilized surroundings, he might find himself an unwelcome guest in his own country. And so, awash in stolen money, Peter Easton set about trying to buy his way back into the good graces of James I. In other words, he was going to purchase a pardon.

Buying a royal pardon was fairly common practice for outlaws in those days—one just had to have enough money. Since applicants for pardons were almost always wanted men, and therefore subject to arrest, the first thing a pardon-seeking outlaw had to find was an emissary, someone to deliver their request to the King's representatives. Easton picked none other than Richard Whitbourne. Perhaps tired of constantly having to deal with a known criminal, Whitbourne set out across the sea to deliver Easton's petition to the Killigrews, who would in turn deliver it to the Royal Court.

As it turned out, Whitbourne needn't have bothered. Leaving nothing to chance, Easton had also sent two other emissaries to the King, each one humbly asking for forgiveness (with a healthy price tag of course). By the time Whitbourne landed in England, the other two messengers had already arrived. King James was no fool when it came to money—when he saw it, he took it. The venerable monarch pardoned Easton not once, but twice, most likely collecting a double fee for so doing. With his past transgressions forgiven,

Easton went straight back to pirating and set about planning the crowning exploit of his ignoble but enviable career.

Every year, a special convoy of Spanish ships set sail from the Caribbean up the coast of North America and then set out across the Atlantic to take the treasures of the New World back to Spain. It was popularly known as the "Spanish Plate Fleet," and every sea-going Englishman knew that it was loaded with fabulous riches of unimaginable splendour and fantastic worth. The Plate Fleet was so called because in olden times, to show off wealth, moneyed families would bedeck the walls of their homes with platters and plates made of gold. Over time, the word "plate" became virtually synonymous with flashy riches—or in modern parlance, "bling."

Through paid informants Easton had discovered when the Spanish Plate Fleet would set out on its journey. He also learned that the fleet would be stopping at the Azore Islands, tiny specks in the Atlantic that were under the rule of Portugal. Like any sailor worth his salt, Easton knew that ships making trans-Atlantic crossings were at the mercy of the currents, huge masses of moving water that carried the ships along with them. Those who sailed against the currents took longer to reach their destinations; those who sailed with them, made record times. Now, leaning over the map table in his cabin, Easton started to form a plan.

He knew that for much of their journey, the Spanish ships would sail atop the churning mass of warm ocean water that is known today as the Gulf Current. It would carry them north, up the eastern coast of North America, and then veer sharply to the east, carrying the treasure-filled ships out into the North Atlantic. From there, they would hitch a ride on the North Atlantic Current, which would carry them more or less towards the Azores.

So far so good, but the challenge of the matter lay in the sheer size of the North Atlantic Current. It was not some piddling stream a mile or two wide, but instead, covered hundreds of miles. This meant that Easton knew more or less where the Plate Fleet was going to wind up, but their approach vector was impossibly wide. For one or two ships it would have been an impossible catch—and, of course, by this time, Easton had more than one or two ships.

His solution reveals something of the spirit of conquest that must have driven him. Not happy to sit back on his laurels, he was willing to take substantial though calculated risks for a chance to win glorious, if ill-gotten gains. And this is exactly what he did. Really, it was surprisingly simple: He put to sea with 14 of his ships, sailed into the Atlantic and had them form a wide semicircle around the southwest radius of the Azores. This way, no matter which direction the Plate Fleet came from, at least one of the pirate ships was sure to spot it and could signal the others.

Not a complicated idea, but one impossible without Easton's substantial pirate fleet. And it worked—the moment one of their number spotted the approaching Spaniards, the pirates pounced. By the time the smoke had cleared, Easton's fleet had captured four Spanish treasure ships, each one stacked to the rails with gold, silver, pearls and emeralds, and each one promising an easy retirement for Easton and his crew.

And that is precisely what Easton did—retire. It is scarcely exaggerating to say that Easton's immense wealth made him, if not the Bill Gates of his era, at least the Donald Trump of his day. After a brief sojourn on the Barbary Coast of Africa, Easton next turned up in 1615 on the Riviera, where he titled himself the "Marquis of Savoy," bought a huge palace and, in Richard Whitbourne's words, "lived rich."

Easton also joined forces with the Duke of Savoy as his "Master of Ordnance," meaning that he was in charge of the big guns, something years of pirating had certainly prepared him well for. He distinguished himself in an attack on the Duchy of Mantua, and after this, he vanishes from the pages of history. Most likely, he went back to the Riviera and enjoyed his loot in lavish style, perhaps pausing once in a while to think fondly back on his days of high-seas piracy.

After he returned from delivering Easton's request for a pardon, Richard Whitbourne went back to working hard, diligently applying himself and eventually becoming a vice-admiralty court judge and Knight of the Realm.

As for Henry Mainwarring, the hot-shot, privateer hired to oust Easton...well, more on him later.

And what of Harbour Grace? Today, the little town still echoes with the battles, adventures and exploits that shook her shores so long ago. In the Pirates' Graveyard, 47 members of Easton's crew still rest in the quiet earth; in 1885 a large anchor, apparently of Spanish design, was discovered, leading many to believe that it was from the *San Sebastien*, captured and burned by Easton's pirates; a small nearby town is named "Happy Adventure," after Easton's flagship; in Harbour Grace stands a monument to Easton's career, and when summer arrives, pirate pageants and re-enactments abound during "Pirates, Buccaneers and Settler Days."

Finally, there is a fact that no one has been able to satisfactorily explain—today, in Conception Bay, there are hundreds of people with the surname "Easton."

Pirates, Privateers and What Else?

Three words that almost mean "pirate."

Buccaneer: During the late 17th century, poachers on Caribbean islands would illegally kill livestock and then smoke the meat on wooden frames called "boucans." Soon locals were calling the thieves "boucaniers," and before long they were applying the term to pirates as well as poachers.

Corsair: So-called because they were associated with specific "courses" (nautical paths), the term "corsair" could apply to either pirates or privateers operating from Africa's Barbary Coast, hence the term "Barbary Corsair."

Swashbuckler: A "buckler" was a small shield carried by swordsmen to ward off the blows of their opponents. To "swash" meant to make a loud noise (presumably by striking your opponent's buckler). Since Elizabethan times, "swashbuckler" has meant a swaggering showoff, possibly one who swashes his own buckler to get the attention of others.

CHAPTER TWO

Henry Mainwarring
and Others

*We hang the petty thieves and appoint the great
ones to public office.*

—Aesop

St. John's, Newfoundland (1614)

Richard Whitbourne, fishing admiral of the port
of St. John's, must have wondered if he was fated
to be a pawn in the hands of pirates and privateers. In 1611 the pirate Peter Easton had begged,
bragged and attempted bribery when he wanted
Whitbourne to provide him with men, supplies
and munitions. Despite the fact that he had no
legal claim to such considerations, Easton had
always projected a distinct air of entitlement—as if
it was his right to receive the favours he sought.

Now, three years later, Whitbourne was faced
with one Henry Mainwarring, a 27-year-old English privateer who positively oozed confidence and
conducted himself in a commanding manner; here
was a man who, even more than Peter Easton,
clearly expected to get his way. Mainwarring's
family was well connected, with many contacts in
the corridors of power and access to people of

influence. His background was one of courtly privilege and impressive achievement. By turns he had been a soldier, a scholar, (at some point) a lawyer and was currently a privateer with letters of marque from King James of England. Henry Mainwarring needed Richard Whitbourne to provide him with men, supplies and munitions, because— and this was the good part—Mainwarring had come to Newfoundland to hunt down and capture none other than Peter Easton.

Mainwarring had only narrowly missed capturing Easton back in England. When he found that his quarry had fled across the Atlantic to Newfoundland, Mainwarring realized that he had a problem. Along with several of his wealthy friends, he had spent a lot of money outfitting three ships as pirate hunters. They had expected to recoup their investment by capturing Easton and laying claim to whatever stolen treasure his fleet happened to be carrying. But now, the big fish had fled the pond, and Mainwarring needed someone, or something, to hunt.

Never one to let facts get in his way, Mainwarring went back to King James and asked for an enlargement of his letters of marque to allow him to hunt not just pirates but also Spaniards. The King granted his request despite the fact that England and Spain were at peace. However, not wanting another naval war on his doorstep, King James stipulated that European waters were off limits, meaning that Mainwarring could only hunt the

Spanish off the coast of Africa or off the shores of
the New World.

Mainwarring promptly sailed for Africa's Barbary Coast to set about attacking and plundering
Spanish ships. At that time the Moors were the
predominant cultural force in North Africa. As a
primarily Muslim culture, the Moors also happened, rather conveniently for Mainwarring, to be
against the Spanish. This meant that he could find
friendly anchorages in the bays and inlets of the
African coast. As Mainwarring raided more and
more Spanish ships, the Moorish rulers took a
genuine shine to him and came to regard him as a
sort of English goodwill Ambassador.

But after two years of this, Mainwarring was in
need of fresh crews and an all around refit of his
ships. It's also likely that the Spanish were on to
him by this point and had started exercising
greater caution in their choice of routes and more
secrecy regarding their schedules. And so, with an
eye to more welcoming waters, Mainwarring
turned his gaze westward.

By this time, Newfoundland was gaining quite a
reputation in the pirating community. Years later,
Mainwarring wrote that it was the best place in the
world to outfit pirate ships. He claimed that many
of the experienced sailors who made their homes
in Newfoundland were eager to throw in their lot
with pirates and willingly joined their crews.
Mainwarring further claimed that he had only
accepted one out of every six men who volunteered

to join him because he did not want to interrupt the smooth functioning of His Majesty's colonial fisheries.

It is worth noting that the person Mainwarring made these claims to was the King himself, and so he had every reason to present himself in a favourable light. His assertion that he had never "enforced" any of his crew members is certainly suspect, though not entirely out of the question. With conflicting claims from contemporary sources, it is difficult to know exactly how many Newfoundlanders willingly joined pirate crews and how many were forced into service.

On the one hand, when thinking of life in a small east-coast fishing community at the turn of the 17th century, "easy" is not the word that leaps to mind. Most potential for either employment or entertainment seems to have centred around fish: catching fish, scaling fish, gutting fish, packing fish in salt—and eating fish for breakfast, lunch and dinner. Then after the day was done, possibly listening to the local minstrels sing a ballad about—what else—fish! Needless to say, if you didn't like the smell of fish, the feel of fish, the sight of fish, the taste of fish, or the sound they made flopping around in a net, you were pretty much out of luck. In circumstances such as these, who *wouldn't* want to join a pirate crew!

On the other hand, it is simply impossible to verify whether or not the pirates who sailed Canada's maritime waters were actually the decent, fair-dealing sorts they sometimes made themselves out to be; they were pirates after all. Certainly many modern-day Canadians would like to imagine that their ancestors could happily have embarked on lives of piracy. But we must remember that for the law-abiding citizens of 17th-century Canada, the word "pirate" likely carried many of the same connotations that the word "terrorist" carries today. It was not necessarily a life that any but the most desperate might aspire to.

Aside from its legions of supposedly willing sailors, Newfoundland also had many other practical features that would appeal to an ambitious and sensible pirate. The first of course was its remoteness; Peter Easton had proven that far from the interfering naval forces of England, France or Spain, pirates could set up entire towns and go about their business of robbing and raiding without worry of interference.

Next, there was an abundance of equipment. As a fishing colony, Newfoundland had all manner of materials on hand to refurbish ships. Pirates could easily lay their hands on rope, sail canvas and other necessities of life at sea. There was also an abundance of food, namely fish. The old saying that an army marches on its stomach is no less true for pirates; a stolen cargo of salted fish would keep for months, giving pirates both a convenient source of travel-ready food as well as valuable cargo that they could trade or sell.

And finally, local officials realized that if they let it be known their colonies were "pirate-friendly," they could put themselves in the way of a good thing. By 1621, Ferryland was being governed by Sir George Calvert, a man who modern historians regard as almost certainly a "fence" for pirates up and down the east coast, discreetly finding buyers and selling their captured booty to the highest bidder.

Henry Mainwarring arrived in Newfoundland on June 4, 1614. Although his letters of marque still identified him as a privateer, he was by this time, for all intents and purposes, a pirate. The arrival of the eight ships must have been an intimidating sight for the locals. Mainwarring's flagship, the *Princess*, led the pack. Painted bright yellow with shining brass hardware and carved wooden scrollwork covered in gold foil, the *Princess* had been fitted with extra decks in her bow and stern to carry additional guns. Her cannons were cast iron, making them the longest shooting and most accurate guns of their age. From her bowsprit were rigged a series of small extra sails that allowed her to make sharp turns at close quarters to outmanoeuver enemy ships. She was indeed a force to be reckoned with.

All this must have crossed Richard Whitbourne's mind as he sat across from Henry Mainwarring and listened to his requests for crewmen and supplies. Aside from his impressive manner and even more impressive firepower, Mainwarring also held

letters of marque signed by the King himself, and
they authorized him to requisition supplies and men
in the King's name. Whitbourne had no way of
knowing that Mainwarring was anything other
than what he claimed to be—a privateer on the
track of Peter Easton (who, by this time, unbe-
knownst to either Whitbourne or Mainwarring, was
on his way to the Azores to plunder the Spanish
Plate Fleet). Given his visitor's impressive creden-
tials, it's likely that Whitbourne gave his distinguished guest all the help he asked for.

According to the Public Records, on September 14,
more than three months after he arrived, Mainwarring left St. John's: "...from all the harbours
whereof they commanded carpenters, maryners,
victuals, munitions.... Of every six maryners they
take one.... From the Portugal ships they took all
their wine...from a French ship in Harbour Grace
they took 10,000 fish...having with them from the
fishing fleet about 400 maryners and fishermen,
many volunteers, many compelled."

From here, Mainwarring took over Peter
Easton's compound at Harbour Grace and raised
merry hell with the Spanish and Portuguese. He
captured ships, seized cargo, stole treasure and
made life generally miserable for honest merchants
flying the flag of either country. So successful was
he that Spain and Portugal complained to King
James, who proceeded to....do nothing.

Once he'd gotten his fill of the New World, Mainwarring sailed back to Europe, at which point the Spanish and Portuguese governments really got angry. They presented a joint petition to the King of England: Unless he declared Henry Mainwarring to be an outlaw and had him arrested, they would consider the peace between their three nations to have been broken, making war a very real possibility.

King James responded by issuing a pardon in Mainwarring's name, absolving him of all wrongdoing (no doubt in return for a substantial bribe). Furthermore, the wayward privateer received a knighthood from his grateful sovereign as well as the command of Dover Castle on England's northern seashore. Here, Mainwarring was elected to Parliament and eventually became a vice admiral in the Royal Navy. From this exalted position he had the nerve to suggest to the King that pirates should no longer receive royal pardons. He also, for the second time in his life, set himself up as a pirate hunter and soon was on the trail of other plundering robbers like himself, which just goes to show that it takes a thief to catch a thief.

Although they were adversaries, Peter Easton and Henry Mainwarring put Newfoundland on the map as a safe haven for pirates, and the following century would see many disciples following in the footsteps of these two pirate pioneers.

100 YEARS LATER, THE GULF OF ST. LAWRENCE (1717)

Pirate captain Peter Bellamy quickly realized that he'd made a terrible error. The ship he'd mistaken for a big merchant hauler with a cargo hold full of valuables wasn't that at all. Oh, she was big all right, of that there was no doubt. But when cannon barrels began to bristle from the openings in her hull, he realized that she was not loaded with wares for trade and commerce—she was actually loaded with guns (36 of them) and soldiers (too many to count) on their way to fortify the walled city of Québec. Now, instead of an easy prize, Bellamy and his crew were in for a tough battle.

Abandoning all thoughts of capturing the ship, Bellamy and his pirates now just wanted to get away. Unfortunately for them, their would-be prey was fast, agile and easily outmanoeuvered them. The captain of the warship wasted no time in putting his 36 guns to good use and opened fire on Bellamy's ship, shredding both her canvas sails and the thick hempen ropes that held them aloft. For the next three hours, thunderous cannonades exploded and echoed across the water as the ships attacked one another, each firing volley after volley at her opponent.

As darkness fell, rain clouds started moving in, and Bellamy took stock of his situation: The damage to his sails and rigging meant that the ship was extremely difficult to control, and 36 of his crewmen were either dead or dying. As the light began to fail, and the smell of approaching rain became stronger, Bellamy finally managed to get away. With his ship badly damaged and a significant number of his crew dead, he had to find somewhere to lick his wounds; the sheltering coast of Newfoundland beckoned.

Hailing from the British Isles, Bellamy had likely been a privateer, licensed by Queen Anne to capture French and Spanish ships. As so often happened before and since, once peace broke out, many privateers turned to piracy. By 1717, three pirate ships under Bellamy's command were prowling the coast of present-day New Brunswick, looking for a good careenage site. A "careenage" was a facility that pirates usually had to improvise, often in a sheltered area where a vessel could be put ashore so that the hull would be exposed at low tide. This allowed the pirates to scrape off the barnacles that stuck to the hull and slowed the ship down, as well as to repair damage the ship might have sustained in battle.

Before his ill-advised encounter with the 36-gun warship, Bellamy had built a careenage in one of the many coves, bays and inlets that notch the coast of New Brunswick. Although its precise location is unknown, by all accounts it was an impressive facility whose purpose went far beyond the maintenance of sailing ships. There was a sizable fort, most likely constructed of earth and wood; its battlements were studded with gun nests and a separate building was built to house gunpowder and other munitions.

The heavy work of building this compound was done by slaves that Bellamy had captured by the boatload in skirmishes off the eastern seaboard and in the Caribbean. As his fortress took shape, the forced labour of the slaves gave him the chance to turn his mind to other things. He made known his grandiose plans to found a new nation with himself as the leader and his lieutenants as a sort of pirate parliament—not so different from how many people view parliaments today.

We can only imagine the names that might have been for this would-be piratocracy: Bellamia, Port Bellamy, Bellamy's Land, The Bay of Bellamy, The Bellamy Coast, Costa Bellamia—the possibilities must have seemed endless. However, being a pirate and not a nation builder, Bellamy set forth once more to plunder the high seas, or at least the Maritimes.

In Newfoundland's Fortune Bay they captured or destroyed several fishing or trading vessels, assimilating many of their crews. Unfortunately, it was after this that Bellamy encountered the 36-gun warship. Having sustained such heavy damage, it was unthinkable to sail all the way back to their old careenage, so Bellamy put his ships ashore somewhere closer: at the west shore of Placentia Bay. Again, the exact location is unknown, but it would have been somewhere remote and easily protected, probably a hidden harbour.

Wherever it was, Bellamy's slaves set busily to work again and soon his ships were once more seaworthy. Sadly, for historians, when he sailed out of this second careenage, he also sailed into the unknown, and nothing more about him can be confirmed. Nor are there any records from this time marking the proclamation of a new pirate republic.

We can only assume that he continued to ply his villainous trade—in both Canadian waters and those beyond.

BONAVISTA BAY, NEWFOUNDLAND (CIRCA 1717)

Captain Woodes Rogers strained his ears in the thick blackness of a moonless night. He and his companions had positioned themselves on a point of land that commanded an excellent view of the narrow channel that led into the harbour of Trinity. The problem was, of course, that without moonlight, the excellent view was no view at all; it was going to be difficult to spot the vessel they were waiting for. They would have to listen for the telltale sounds that might betray the ship's passing: a sound from the sailors on board, a breath of wind through the rigging or the creaking of the ship itself.

Rogers' cohorts were sea captains like himself, and at this point all of them were angry and determined. A few days earlier they had been ashore in Trinity, going about their lawful business as their ships lay at anchor in the harbour. Most of them were fishing vessels whose crews were at work on shore, leaving the ships virtually unmanned. And then, with little or no fanfare, a single-masted sloop entered the harbour and sailed from ship to ship, putting crews aboard to take whatever they desired. Finally, the little pirate vessel sailed up to the mighty *Herman*, a much larger ship with 24 guns to the sloop's 12. And here, the pirates stopped. They too put down anchor and set about transferring weapons, supplies and stolen goods onto their new flagship— the *Herman*. Meanwhile, all the rightful captains and crews could do was watch from shore, grinding their teeth and swearing under their breath.

But Captain Rogers hatched a plot to recapture the *Herman*—he and his fellow captains had found a few ships' guns that were being stored on shore in the town. And everyone knew that there was an abandoned fort out on the point, looking across the channel. As the pirates brazenly refitted their new flagship in full view of her rightful masters, Rogers and his cohorts dragged the guns over to the fort, mounted them, and aimed them into the channel. Then as night fell, they settled down to wait, no doubt cursing some more when the clouds drifted in to blot out the moon.

At last someone must have heard something—either a careless voice or maybe the lapping of water against the hull—for the inky stillness of the night was abruptly split open by the lightning flash of the first shot and the booming thunder of its echo. With no moon to light their target, Rogers and his gunner captains had to aim by sheer guesswork—and they were reasonably successful, reporting that they heard many sounds of impact as their shots crashed into the hull of the *Herman*.

But in this case, luck did not favour the brave, and the *Herman* slipped past the town guardians to set sail for the open sea.

The *Herman*'s new master was a pirate known to history only as Captain Lewis (first name unknown). Lewis' place of birth is also unknown, but by the age of 10 he was serving in some capacity on a pirate ship operating near Jamaica. When an English warship captured the pirates, her captain ordered them all to be hanged, except Lewis and another child discovered on board. Thoroughly terrified by his brush with execution (and roughing up at the hands of the English sea captain who hung him by the waist from a yard arm), Lewis went into honest service as a ship's boy and later, an ordinary seaman.

But soon, Lewis' ship was captured by Spaniards and taken to Cuba where Lewis was enslaved by his Spanish masters for several years. Finally, along with some fellow slaves, he stole a canoe and escaped to Cuba's coastal region. Here the fugitives organized themselves to begin stealing guns and supplies from the local plantations. When at last they had acquired ample weapons and steady nerves, they captured a sloop and became pirates, electing Lewis as their captain, not only because he was an able leader but probably also because he spoke English, Spanish and French.

From Cuba they sailed north, doing a bit of pirating off the coast of Florida before heading to Newfoundland.

After his narrow escape from Woodes Rogers, Captain Lewis captured a large French ship off the coast of Newfoundland and sent half of his crew to man her. He now had three ships: the *Herman*, the new French prize and his original sloop. And just as he collected ships, so had he gathered men, amassing an unruly band of French and English high-seas desperadoes. The fleet sailed for Africa where they lurked off the coast, capturing many English, Dutch and Portuguese ships. Eventually, Lewis commanded so many ships that he could send off three or four at a time to conduct raids, each manned by a hodgepodge of nationalities, mainly French and English.

Knowing that Lewis' crews were French and English, and bearing in mind that this book is about *Canadian* pirates, what happened next should come as no surprise: Friction arose between the French and English factions. What they squabbled about remains unknown, though possibly the French pirates grew tired of the English pirates giving orders in English all the time, and possibly the English pirates grew tired of the French pirates going on about this at such great length and in French only. At any rate, finally these two groups *separated*, each taking their own ships and sailing off to their different fates—or at least that was how it was supposed to work.

The lesson (if any) to be learned here is that separation does not lead to harmony. After all, piracy is a highly competitive venture; there's only so much treasure to go around and the ocean is awfully big, so if you're running short on supplies and you happen to come upon your former fellow pirates—why not just take *their* provisions? The separate French and English fleets, formerly united under Captain Lewis' command, now started attacking one another. They chased each other around the east Atlantic until at last, in one of these raids, Lewis was killed. After this his crews gradually fell apart, proving that even pirates fall divided.

Charles Bellamy and Captain Lewis took full advantage of the many qualities that made Newfoundland attractive to pirates. But all the while, the really hot action was happening down south in the waters of the Caribbean and off the shores of the Spanish Main. Here, not only could pirates take advantage of busy shipping lanes full of prosperous traders, but they could also enjoy the warm weather. The move, however, had its drawbacks. As soon as a place was popular for pirates, it often became more heavily patrolled by warships seeking to maintain order. Not only were there rival pirates to contend with, but also heavily armed representatives of sovereign nations who tended to shoot first and ask questions later. In the summer months, therefore, some pirates realized that they might do well to head north, where the waters were just a little less crowded and the competition perhaps a little less intense. And in the summer of 1720, the captain known as the greatest pirate of them all did just that.

CHAPTER THREE

Bartholomew Roberts
(aka "Black Bart")

...a merry life and a short one shall be my motto.

–B.R.

BARTHOLOMEW ROBERTS, BETTER KNOWN AS "BLACK BART," is rightly regarded as one of the most successful pirates of his day, capturing a staggering 400 vessels in a career that lasted barely three years. He also fits right in with most people's idea of a pirate captain: he was alternately loved and feared by his men and was recognized as a fair master, but one with a murderous temper. He put the torch to a boatload of captive slaves, burning them alive. He flogged prisoners nearly to death, cut off their ears, strung them from the yard arm and used them for target practice.

He dressed flamboyantly and is known to have sailed into battle dressed in blood-red garments of the finest damask, wearing a diamond-studded cross hung from a solid gold chain, all topped off with a peacock-plumed hat. Though he was born in Wales and menaced the waters on both sides of the Atlantic, he is particularly well remembered in Trepassey, Newfoundland, for it was here that he conducted one of the most notorious pirate raids in Canadian history.

TREPASSEY HARBOUR, NEWFOUNDLAND (JUNE 21, 1720)

The bone-rattling crack of cannon fire shook the air, and residents of the little fishing village rushed to windows, scurried into streets and squinted from the ends of docks. They peered out into the harbour trying to see what was happening, but a fishing fleet of 22 ships had recently put in and the floating forest of their masts obscured the view. There were also at least 250 smaller boats moored or docked, and all of them made it hard to see. What was going on?

The cannonade continued, a chain of booming explosions, each one making the onlookers feel as though an invisible hand with an open palm had thumped them on the chest. And what was that between the blasts—was it…music? Surely that was the keening slice of fiddle strings drifting over the water. And was that the brassy trumpeting sound of…horns?

And then, through a gap in the smoke, someone saw the flag, a black rectangle of cloth snapping in the wind. At its centre was the white figure of a pirate with his sword drawn. He stood, ready for a fight, each foot planted firmly on a white skull. Under the skull on the left were the letters "ABH"; on the right, "AMH." Even the villagers who couldn't read knew how to recognize letters, and these ones sent a chill down their spines. "ABH" stood for "A Barbadian's Head," and "AMH" stood for "A Martinican's Head." The man who flew this flag was known far and wide for his vicious cruelty; hunted in both Barbados and Martinique, he was openly advertising his consuming hatred for the countries who wanted his capture. The townsfolk stood aghast as they realized that the dreaded pirate Bartholomew Roberts had just sailed into their harbour, guns blazing.

Although he'd been a pirate for barely a year, Black Bart was fast becoming a seasoned pro. From previous engagements he knew that if he struck boldly and without warning, his chances of success were much greater. Off the Brazilian coast he had sailed his ship, the *Royal Rover*, straight into the middle of 42 Portuguese merchant ships and dropped anchor as though he were part of the fleet. Next, he cordially invited one of the Portuguese captains on board, then calmly explained that unless his captive guest told him which ship was laden with the most riches, he would kill him. Once the terrified captain had named a ship, Roberts sailed over to her and opened fire, disabling his prey with a single volley. His crew boarded the captured vessel, efficiently looted its cargo of gold, sugar and tobacco, transferred their newfound riches to the *Rover* and sailed away before the two warships guarding the fleet could get close enough to do anything.

But this early success did Roberts and his men little good. Although they were rich in loot, they were running low on water and food. So Roberts and some of his men took one of the single-masted sloops they'd captured and gave chase to a brigantine that looked like easy pickings. When the brigantine easily outran them, they returned to where they'd left the *Rover* only to discover that the rest of the pirates had sailed off without them, absconding with not only the ship but also the treasure.

Roberts quickly captured two more sloops and used these to board a much larger merchant ship from Bristol, stealing all of her provisions and then letting her go. A few days later, feeling more confident, he made towards two sloops that seemed like sitting ducks—the *Summerset* and the *Philipa*, both out of Barbados. We can only imagine how quickly his anticipation turned to alarm as he realized that far from being peaceable merchants, the sloops were heavily armed gun ships both intent on hunting him down.

For the next two hours, cannon shots and gunfire exploded in the Caribbean sunshine. At last though, with 20 of his crew severely injured, Roberts turned tail and sailed off into the afternoon. His plan was to head to Dominica to repair his ships and re-provision, but he soon found that the nearby island of Martinique had also sent out ships to hunt him. When all of his wounded men died from their injuries, Roberts decided that the warm southern waters had become too hot; perhaps there was easier hunting to be had to the north.

And so he set sail up the coast and, although he didn't know it, his first port of call would be Ferryland—the little town that 100 years before had been home base to his pirate predecessor, Peter Easton.

When he spied the bristling masts in Trepassey Harbour, Roberts must have smiled. It had been easy at Ferryland; he'd captured 12 ships there and realized that these little isolated fishing villages were virtually defenceless. They were inhabited by law-abiding folk trying to make an honest living from the bounty of the sea and not inclined to put up a fight. Their ships and stores were ripe for gutting, like the fat bellies of so many fish.

Roberts' current ship was called the *Fortune*, and now he ordered the gunners to pack her cannons with gunpowder, but not to bother with any shot. After all, he just wanted to frighten his victims, not destroy the ships he intended to rob. He also ordered the ship's minstrels on deck and instructed them to play loudly and with much passion. Not all pirate crews included musicians, but most captains knew that music was a good way to boost a crew's spirits during tough times or long periods of boredom. And in surprise attacks like this one, the combination of cannon fire and the raucous minstrel show created a chaotic, confusing atmosphere.

It also sent the message that for the pirates, murder and mayhem went hand in hand with having a good time. Mixed with the booming of the cannons, the frenzied scratch of the fiddle and the bombastic notes of the horn seemed to say, "Raise your voices in protest and we shall laughingly cut out your tongues. Raise your hands against us and we shall merrily cut off your arms—all the while humming a happy tune."

The mingled horror and surprise of the people watching from shore was nothing compared to the naked terror of those on the ships anchored in the harbour. News of Black Bart's dire deeds had spread far and wide—everyone knew his reputation for wanton cruelty and savage violence. By some accounts he had even sent a messenger ahead to warn the inhabitants of Trepassey that he was coming. Not surprisingly, the captains and crews of the fishing fleet couldn't abandon ship fast enough. Some leapt into the water and swam ashore while others embarked in small boats and frantically rowed themselves out of harm's way. Most prominently, a chubby shipowner known as Admiral Babidge, one of the richest men in Newfoundland, was seen to abandon his magnificent vessel, the *Bideford*, and make for shore with unseemly haste.

Silencing his guns, Roberts dropped anchor and instructed his men to take what they might from the abandoned ships, starting with the *Bideford*. The pirate boarding party hauled down the captive ship's flag and then turned her big guns on the town, destroying a few of the buildings. Then they cut down the masts and slashed the rigging of several of the larger ships; this would prevent their rightful owners from escaping in their vessels or sailing them against the invaders.

The crowds cowered on the shore, watching the pirates wreck their ships and bombard their homes. For his part, Roberts was disgusted at the way the ships' masters had abandoned their own vessels (even though that was what he'd wanted them to do). His bile was further raised by the fact that no one in the town seemed to have enough backbone to fire a single shot at him or his men. After all, Trepassey had shore guns like any coastal settlement, and many of the ships in harbour were much larger and more heavily armed than the *Fortune*. Roberts' boarding party had even found the *Bideford*'s guns loaded, primed and ready to fire. Not only that, he had given them two days' notice that he was coming—they should have put up a fight!

Roberts moved the *Fortune* into position at the end of the narrow bay leading to Trepassey Harbour. Any ship seeking to enter the harbour had to first pass through the narrow channel, making it the perfect place to lie in wait for unsuspecting prey. With almost leisurely ease, Roberts' men captured four more ships, bringing their total take for the day to 26: the 22 vessels moored in the harbour and the four they'd taken at the mouth of the channel.

Roberts was also mulling over ways to make the town's masters pay for their cowardly behaviour.

At the end of the day, the *Fortune* sailed back into the harbour, and Roberts ordered all of Trepassey's captains to come aboard. He started by singling out the portly Admiral Babidge, who had been so quick to abandon his ship. He had Babidge tied to the *Fortune*'s mast with his wrists above his head and then flogged him until Babidge's silk shirt fell in tatters from his bloodied back. For good measure he had some of the other captains whipped as well. Then he explained how the next few days were going to unfold. Every morning, he would fire the *Fortune*'s gun, and upon hearing this, all of the ships' captains would row out to the *Fortune* to meet with him. Any captain who failed to do so would find his ship burnt; it wasn't a threat but simply a statement of fact.

And as June wore on, this is exactly what happened. For the most part, Roberts picked one or two captains every day and ordered them to take his men aboard their ships to show them where anything of value was kept or hidden. He also appears to have spent a lot of time trying on the many fine garments and accoutrement that came his way from the captured vessels. As well as coats, cravats and breeches, Roberts also acquired at least one set of fine china to drink his tea from. As for his crew, when the day's work was done, they went ashore in marauding groups of 40 to 50 and terrorized the town in a drunken rampage of rape, pillage and random pistol fire.

Of the many sturdy ships in the harbour, one in particular caught Black Bart's eye—she was a square-rigged two-master from Bristol. More importantly, she was also fitted with oars, making travel still possible even without wind, and allowing her to be easily manoeuvered in narrow channels or inlets. The ship's former owner, a man named Copleston, had to watch as the vessel that had once been his pride and joy was now refitted as Roberts' new pirate flagship, eventually being rechristened, the *Good Fortune*. The other captains, all 20-odd of them, watched as their own ships were stripped of anything useful and left floating sadly at anchor. From shore the bare masts of the ships loomed forlornly like straight, dark cuts in the sky.

Bartholomew Roberts had never wanted to be a pirate. In 1719, at the age of 37, he was working as the third mate of a slave ship called the *Princess*. He was smart, tough and had gained a reputation as an excellent navigator. He seems to have resigned himself to a lackluster fate; that is, he might eventually be promoted to first mate, but unless he actually owned a ship himself (which was unlikely), he could never hope for a captaincy.

One day though, as she lay anchored off the coast of Africa, the *Princess* was captured by another famous pirate, Howell Davis. He took the entire crew prisoner and pressed them into service on his own ship. Good navigators were hard to find, and Davis quickly realized that Roberts would make a valuable addition to his permanent crew. Although Roberts resented being forced to join a crew of pirates, he signed on anyway, probably under threat of death from Davis if he refused. When Davis was killed a few weeks later in a botched attempt to kill the governor of the Island of Princes (now called Principe), the pirate crew found themselves without a leader.

The command structure of a pirate ship was surprisingly democratic: Captains were usually elected and then "Articles of Agreement" were drawn up outlining the rules of the ship. The captain was given certain privileges, such as a larger share of treasure as well as the use of the "great cabin" at the stern of the ship, but he was always aware that he was at the mercy of the men he commanded. According to a famous 18th century book, *The General History of the Pyrates*, a pirate crew would elect a captain "on Condition that they may be Captain over him; they separate to his Use the great Cabin,...but then every Man, as the Humour takes him, will...intrude into his Apartment, swear at him, seize a Part of his Victuals and Drink, if they like it, without his offering to find Fault or contest it."

As the surviving members of Captain Davis' crew gathered to pick a new leader, one of the elders stepped forward and made a short speech:

> *If one should be elected who did not act and govern for the general good, he could be deposed and another one substituted in his place...and should a captain be so saucy as to exceed prescription at any time, why, down with him!..... it is my advice, while we are sober, to pitch upon a man of courage, and skilled in navigation, - one who, by his prudence seems best able to defend...us from the dangers and tempests of an unstable element... and such a one I take Roberts to be. A fellow in all respects worthy of your esteem and favor.*

Incredibly, the pirates were nominating Roberts—a man who had been in their crew for less than two months and who didn't want to be a pirate—as their captain! Perhaps even more incredibly, Roberts accepted, reasoning that if he had to be a pirate he would rather lead than follow. He lost no time in drawing up new Articles of Agreement to set out the rules of conduct that would govern the lives of his pirate crew. These rules (and the strong hand of a firm captain) were the social contract that prevented pirate bands from degenerating into complete chaos. Roberts' articles in particular provide an intimate window into daily life on a pirate ship.

1. *Every man shall have an equal vote in affairs of moment. He shall have an equal title to the fresh provisions or strong liquors at any time seized, and shall use them at pleasure unless a scarcity may make it necessary for the common good that a retrenchment may be voted.*

   (Every man had free run of grub and grog unless there was a shortage.)

2. *Every man shall be called fairly in turn by the list on board of prizes, because over and above their proper share, they are allowed a shift of clothes. But if they defraud the company to the value of even one dollar in plate, jewels or money, they shall be marooned. If any man rob another he shall have his nose and ears slit, and be put ashore where he shall be sure to encounter hardships.*

   (Each man was entitled to his share of treasure, plus a change of clothes, but thieves would be dealt with harshly. "Marooning" meant putting a man ashore on a deserted island and leaving him there. Mutilating the faces of thieves not only served as gruesome punishment but also branded them forever as being untrustworthy.)

3. *None shall game for money either with dice or cards.*

   (No gambling!)

4. *The lights and candles should be put out at eight at night, and if any of the crew desire to drink after that hour they shall sit upon the open deck without lights.*

(Drunkenness was a constant problem on most pirate ships and Roberts' fleet was no exception. Apparently one of his crew became so incapacitated by drink that he had to be hoisted off the ship with a block and tackle. Roberts himself seems to have enjoyed the occasional glass of beer but usually preferred to take tea in his cabin. For the most part he was quite temperate compared to his constantly sozzled crew.)

5. *Each man shall keep his piece, cutlass and pistols at all times clean and ready for action.*

(Like any fighting force, pirate crews had to be battle-ready at a moment's notice, and so clean, well-maintained weapons were a must.)

6. *No boy or woman to be allowed amongst them. If any man shall be found seducing any of the latter sex and carrying her to sea in disguise he shall suffer death.*

(This rule arose not from any prudishness on the part of pirates, but rather, the well-founded fear that shipboard bedmates would give rise to jealousy and competition among the men, so disrupting the solidarity of the crew.)

7. *He that shall desert the ship or his quarters in time of battle shall be punished by death or marooning.*

(It was the unwritten law that in times of battle, the crew had to unquestioningly obey the captain's every order, and so desertion during battle would have been a particularly offensive breach of duty.)

8. *None shall strike another on board the ship, but every man's quarrel shall be ended on shore by sword or pistol in this manner. At the word of command from the quartermaster, each man being previously placed back to back, shall turn and fire immediately. If any man do not, the quartermaster shall knock the piece out of his hand. If both miss their aim they shall take to their cutlasses, and he that draweth first blood shall be declared the victor.*

(All quarrels had to be settled on shore, the pirate equivalent of facing off in the schoolyard at recess. If neither combatant had managed to wound the other with pistols at 10 paces, then they had to fight it out with swords. When his temper was up, Roberts himself ignored this rule, once shooting a crewman dead right on the ship's deck.)

9. *No man shall talk of breaking up their way of living till each has a share of 1,000. Every man who shall become a cripple or lose a limb in the service shall have 800 pieces of eight from the common stock and for lesser hurts proportionately.*

(This suggests that no pirate would be allowed to leave the crew until he had amassed at least 1000 treasure shares. If he was injured, a sort of on-board "insurance policy" [see end of this chapter] would be awarded.)

10. *The captain and the quartermaster shall each receive two shares of a prize, the master gunner and boat- swain one and one half shares, all other officers one*

and one quarter, and private gentlemen of fortune one share each.

(The higher your rank, the more shares of treasure you were entitled to.)

11. *The musicians shall have rest on the Sabbath Day only by right. On all other days by favor only.*

(This article has led many to believe that Roberts was a pious, God-fearing pirate, but there is little evidence that he feared anyone, least of all God. More likely, he realized that since the musicians were on call 24 hours a day, they needed some time to rest.)

Black Bart enforced or ignored these rules at his pleasure and was very much his own man when it came to his style of captaincy. To begin with, he was apparently a harsher and more authoritarian captain than many of his peers. It is difficult to imagine him allowing the crew to burst into his cabin and help themselves to his food and drink or jovially curse him. He also kept to himself, rarely socializing with his crew, preferring his own company. Moreover, he dressed like a dandy and was oft seen clad in costly garments, cut from the finest materials that stolen money could buy. This would further set him apart from his underlings who most likely went barefoot and dressed for function rather than fashion.

Black Bart was probably such a lone wolf for two reasons: First, he was better educated than most of his crew, being able to read, write and navigate.

Second, he was likely always resentful at being forced into leading a bunch of cutthroats with whom he had little in common. However, Roberts eventually came round to a more favourable view of his new lifestyle, reputedly saying, "In an honest service there is...low wages, and hard labour. In this, plenty and satiety, pleasure and ease, liberty and power.... No, a merry life for me and a short one shall be my motto."

As the month of June neared its end, the refit of the *Good Fortune* was complete. After seven long days at the mercy of Bartholomew Roberts, Trepassey was ready to be left in peace, but that is not what happened. On the day he put to sea, Roberts had his men set fire to every ship in the harbour and, by some accounts, most of the buildings on shore as well; in short, anything that would burn. The black plume of smoke spiraling skyward was seen as far as 13 miles away in Cape Pine. As Roberts' forces made their grand exit, he may have ordered the musicians on deck to play the ships out of the harbour and back to the open sea, tapping his toes as the town behind him burned. If you were looking astern at an entire harbour in flames, it was easy to imagine that Bartholomew Roberts had just thrown open the gates of hell itself.

Later that year, an English newspaper, *The Weekly Journal or British Gazetteer*, summarized Roberts' Newfoundland adventures with a paragraph that scarcely does justice to the horrors he inflicted:

> *St Lawrence. 28 June. A pirate in a small sloop of 12 guns and 160 men entered Trepassey on Tuesday the 21st inst, and made himself master of the said harbour and of all the ships there, being 22 sail and 250 shallops. He made the masters all prisoners and beat some of them heartily for their cowardice for not making any resistance. The Admiral, one Babidge, in the Bideford Merchant, suffered most because he and all his hands left their ship with jack, ensign and pendent flying, his guns all loaden in order to defend themselves but the pirate was close alongside him, struck his colours, hoisted their own and fired all his guns. They cut his masts and several others close by the deck. He cut all the other ships cables in junks and their shrouds. He seized one Copleston's ship for himself and set all the ships carpenters to work to fit her for his purpose. He threatened to burn all the rest and to hang one of the masters at least for their incivility in not waiting upon him to make him welcome at his entrance. he destroyed about 30 sail, French and English, on the Banks.*

Black Bart's Canadian adventures weren't quite over yet. After putting the torch to Trepassey, he headed for Nova Scotia and captured at least six large French vessels, one of which was so grand that she became the new *Good Fortune*. Then Roberts raided Cape Breton, abducted several of the French colonists and proceeded to flog them, cut off their ears and hanged them, still living, from the yard arm for casual musket practice. He prowled the Atlantic, capturing ship after ship, leaving a trail of blood in his wake. In Martinique, he hoisted flags that falsely identified him as a peaceful trader, then destroyed 20 small vessels that sailed out to trade with him.

He kidnapped the governor of Martinique and did with him as he had done with the Cape Breton Frenchmen. He captured a ship with 80 slaves on board and set it aflame; the slaves, chained below decks, were burned alive. After three years of rampant piracy, homicidal bloodshed and general mayhem, more than one sea-going nation wanted Black Bart's head—or at least to see his dead body swinging in irons, his eyes and skin eaten away by crows.

The end came amid thunder, lightning and crashing seas as Roberts fought a pitched battle in the waters of the South Indies. An English warship, the *Swallow*, surprised Roberts' flagship, the *Great Ranger*, just as a huge storm broke. Roberts put on his best clothes and went on deck to greet the enemy and to face the storm. With his customary bravado, Roberts sailed straight into the teeth of the oncoming flotilla. But within minutes the Ranger's sails were shredded by the *Swallow's* guns, and the ship was at the mercy of the waves.

With the *Ranger's* sails destroyed, Captain Ogle of the *Swallow* turned his guns on the pirates themselves. Roberts is reported to have been hit in the throat, crashing to the deck with blood bubbling out of his mangled gullet.

When the authorities killed a wanted pirate, they subjected the corpse to all kinds of indignities: Usually the body was encased in a closely fitted iron cage and hung aloft in some public place for all to see. As the body decomposed, birds and insects would pick the flesh from the skeleton, finally leaving a withered bag of bones that served as a grisly reminder to would-be pirates that this too could be their fate.

Knowing this full well, Roberts had issued standing orders to his crew that should he be killed, they must immediately throw his body overboard so that he could not be made an example of. And that is exactly what they did, some even weeping as they heaved the lifeless body that had once been their captain over the rail and into the sheltering waves.

The death of Bartholomew Roberts marked the end of the so-called "Golden Age of Pirates." With more and more countries making concerted efforts to hunt down and punish pirates, life under the black flag had simply become too risky. Pirates who captured ships and raided settlements ashore could soon expect to find official warships bearing down on them. Rampant piracy even gave rise to a new breed of privateers whose letters of marque bid them specifically to hunt down and kill pirates. All of these factors combined to make pirating much less attractive and much more dangerous. The seven seas were slowly becoming safer.

But all of this was cold comfort to the merchants of Trepassey, Newfoundland, and the many other victims of the dreaded pirate Roberts.

An Arm and a Leg:
What loss of limb was worth.

A pirate ship's "Articles of Agreement" would often spell out how much money the injured crew members were eligible to receive if they lost limbs in the course of action. It was an early form of insurance.

Right Arm:	600 pieces of eight
Left Arm:	500 pieces of eight
Right Leg:	500 pieces of eight
Left Leg:	400 pieces of eight
Eye or Finger:	100 pieces of eight

CHAPTER FOUR

Pirate Fact vs. Pirate Fiction

Truthiness: to know something intuitively, instinctively or "from the gut" without regard to evidence, logic or actual facts.

−coined by comedian Stephen Colbert

UTTER THE WORD "PIRATE" AND PEOPLE WILL THINK OF ALL sorts of things: wooden legs, three-masted ships, squawking parrots on shoulders, chests brimming with gold, buried treasure, maps with "X" marking the spot, eye patches and, of course, black flags with white skulls and crossbones.

But where do these notions come from? Are any of them historically accurate? The commonly held pop-culture image of a pirate (Canadian or otherwise) is an uneven mixture of historical fact and wishful fiction. Surprisingly though, some of the most outrageous stereotypes come the closest to being true, while seemingly more mundane assumptions turn out to be false.

A work that will come up again and again in this chapter is the novel *Treasure Island*, written by Robert Louis Stevenson and first published in 1881. Many details in the story echo the characters and exploits of famous real-life pirates like Blackbeard and Captain Kidd, but Stevenson also wove many threads of pure imagination into this wonderful book.

It was *Treasure Island* that first introduced readers to one-legged, parrot-shouldered Long John Silver. He is searching for a dead man's chest full of pieces of eight, which is hidden somewhere on Skeleton Island. He desperately needs to find a long-lost treasure map on which "X" marks the spot. Treasure Island was a huge success when it came out, and 50 years later Hollywood adopted many of the ideas and images the book had popularized. So we owe our knowledge of pirates to a novel published more than one hundred years ago and to countless movies—but how much of it is true?

Imagine, if you will, the following scene:

A three-masted pirate ship sails the seas when suddenly it happens upon another vessel. The pirates hoist the Jolly Roger, then sail into battle. Their cannonballs lay waste to the ship, smashing its hull to pieces. Then a band of peg-legged pirates with parrots on their shoulders swarm aboard, growling "Arrr" in broad English accents, wielding curved, shining cutlasses and carrying six pistols apiece. They conduct a speedy raid, rob the ship of its precious treasure and make unwilling victims walk the plank. Then they bury their loot and make an elaborate map with a large "X" marking the spot. After this they sail off into the sunset.

The little story above is certainly ridiculous, but it does contain most of the stereotypes that many people associate with pirates. To find out how many of them have a basis in truth, let us begin at the beginning:

Types of Vessels: "A three-masted pirate ship..."

During the age of piracy, the word "ship" specifically meant a three-masted vessel with square-rigged sails. Although a few pirates, like Peter Easton and Bartholomew Roberts, actually did sail in "ships," the majority of pirates sailed in "sloops," which were much smaller and only had one mast. But for early Hollywood directors, ships were much more interesting to look at because they had three masts. They may have also been borrowing a page from *Treasure Island* in which the *Hispanolia* is a sinister pirate schooner. A "schooner" also has three masts but is different from a ship because of the way its sails are rigged.

Hunting Methods: "...suddenly it happens upon another vessel."

Luck and chance certainly were a part of pirate raids, but the most successful pirates actually stalked their prey. Like Peter Easton, they might lurk in busy shipping lanes, waiting for a particular ship or fleet. If they were near a coastline they knew well, they could hide in inlets and bays to ambush their victims. Pirates would also gather as much information as possible before deciding to go on the attack. They might hang around in the bars and coffee-houses of busy port towns, hoping to find answers to questions such as: How large a crew did the target ship have? What was its cargo? How many cannons were on board?

And when they were lucky enough to just happen across a ship at sea, pirates still had to determine if she was actually carrying anything of value. Ships riding low in the water were usually full of cargo. Ones that rode high in the water were probably empty and therefore not good targets— unless of course the pirates were simply after a new ship.

Pirate Flags and Insignia: "The pirates hoist the Jolly Roger..."

The Jolly Roger, with its grinning white skull and crossbones on a black background, is an icon of piratedom. *Treasure Island* injected this image into the mainstream (though earlier works of fiction had mentioned it), and Hollywood happily followed suit, usually showing all pirate ships flying this same flag. But in reality, each pirate captain had his own separate and distinctive insignia. Some flags showed an entire skeleton, whereas others combined skulls or bones with symbols like hourglasses, bleeding hearts, darts, swords and spears. The idea was to show victims that their time was limited and their deaths would be violent. Most feared of all were flags with red backgrounds, since pirates who flew them were signalling an intent to kill everyone they encountered.

Use of Cannons: "Their cannonballs lay waste to the ship, smashing its hull to pieces."

If attacking pirates were angry or impatient, then they might actually shoot to destroy. But many captains tried to do as little damage as possible so that they had the option of adding captured ships to the pirate fleet. The easiest way to hobble a ship without destroying it was to shred the sails, which required weapons more specialized than simple cannonballs. "Bag-shot" was a leather pouch of metal pellets that could be fired from a cannon and acted like a shotgun blast, with the pellets expanding in flight, thus able to shred sail canvas without knocking over the mast.

"Chain-shot" consisted of two cannonballs attached together with a length of chain; in flight, the differing trajectories of the two balls would pull the chain taut, making a larger projectile. Finally, "bar-shot" was made up of two cannonballs attached by a solid bar of metal; in flight, the whole thing would spin around, puncturing a larger hole in sail than a mere cannonball.

Missing Limbs and Exotic Birds: "...a band of peg-legged pirates with parrots on their shoulders..."

It is in *Treasure Island* that we first meet one-legged, parrot-sporting ship's cook, Long John Silver. Wacky as this image may seem, Robert Louis Stevenson was actually on firm footing here (so to speak), since veteran pirates (and many honest sailors) were often missing limbs that had been lost in battle. Even though the fictional Silver has a crutch instead of an actual wooden leg, an engraving from 1780 shows a "Sea Cook" with the unmistakable peg of a wooden leg showing beneath the hem of his pants. There are other historical accounts that also specifically mention pirates with wooden legs.

And what about the parrot? Widely travelled sailors often kept parrots as souvenirs because they were brightly coloured, could be taught to talk and didn't take up much room in the cramped confines of a ship. Long John Silver's parrot is named Cap'n Flint, and throughout the book he shrieks "Pieces of Eight" at the top of his avian lungs. Although Silver keeps him in a cage most of the time, Cap'n Flint also likes to preen his feathers as he sits on Silver's shoulder. In reality, parrots are quite smart and can be taught to obey certain commands. It is easy to imagine bored pirates teaching their parrots to hop up on their shoulders as a way to while away long hours at sea.

Pirate-Speak: "...swarm aboard growling 'Arrr' in broad English accents..."

The outrageous English accents that we assume all pirates must have spoken with—the one with the rounded R's of "Arr!"—can almost certainly be traced to the inspired performance of Robert Newton as Long John Silver in the 1954 film adaptation of Treasure Island. Newton was from Dorset, England, and played the part of Long John Silver with his natural "West Country" accent. He was such a success that he went on to play Silver again in the sequel and yet again in a 13-part miniseries. He is recognized as having set the gold standard for all subsequent portrayals of pirates (for more on Pirate-Speak, see the Glossary at the end of the book).

Weapons: "...wielding curved, shining cutlasses and carrying six pistols apiece..."

Pirates often were armed to the teeth—and with good reason. Early single-shot pistols were unreliable, meaning that right in the middle of a raid, pirates might find their weapons going "click" instead of "bang." The obvious solution was to carry more than one gun, and though not every pirate carried six, those who could afford to seem to have packed more than a couple.

Another important weapon for ship-to-ship raids was a primitive form of grenade. In most cases these were small glass bottles packed with gunpowder and shot, sealed with wax, ignited by rudimentary fuses and then lobbed onto the deck of nearby ships. Not only were they destructive and deadly, but they also caused confusion and tended to frighten the enemy into submission. Of course, swords, axes, clubs and other instruments of blunt trauma were also tools of the trade for a well-armed pirate.

Raiding Techniques: "They conduct a speedy raid, rob the ship of its precious treasure…"

Some pirates attacks were speedy, but just as often, once the pirates had subdued the crew, they would stay on board for as long as it took to find the treasure. And if they couldn't frighten or torture any of the prisoners into telling them where the loot was hidden, this could take quite a while. Bartholomew Roberts' pirates once lingered for nearly two days as they ransacked a ship off the coast of Newfoundland. Even if they didn't find any actual treasure, most pirate crews weren't disappointed to come across more mundane items, such as food, clothes and even spare rope or sail for their ship.

Punishment and Persuasion: "…make unwilling victims walk the plank."

There is only one documented case of pirates making someone walk the plank, and it happens more often in fiction than fact. Truth be known, someone made to walk the plank would have been getting off easy because most pirates practised far more creative forms of killing and torture. These might include inserting lit matches into the eye sockets, pulling out internal organs while the victim was conscious, hacking off limbs and other body parts (including, in one case, the victim's lips), and finally, "woolding," a gruesome process in which a rope was tightened around the victim's head until the unfortunate soul's eyeballs popped out.

Buried Treasure and Treasure Maps: "Then they bury their loot and make an elaborate map with a large 'X' marking the spot."

There are very few documented cases of pirates burying treasure, and even then usually only if the authorities or rival thieves were in hot pursuit. In these cases, it was almost immediately dug up once the danger had passed. The fact of the matter is that when pirates captured a boatload of loot, their top priority was to sell it off as fast as they could, thereby converting their spoils into cash.

When Robert Louis Stevenson spun the tail of *Treasure Island*, he may have been influenced by the legends of a vast treasure buried by Captain Kidd, who was active near the turn of the 18th century. When Kidd was arrested, there was a huge discrepancy between the treasure he is alleged to have stolen and the treasure that the authorities could account for. He had also hidden much of his treasure not by burying it, but simply leaving it for safekeeping with family and friends in three different corners of the globe. We will never know the true value of Kidd's takings, but their rumoured splendour will fuel the dreams of treasure hunters for years to come.

What about treasure maps then? If there was no buried treasure, why do maps marked with an "X" loom so prominently in pirate lore? Appropriately enough, mapping an imaginary island was what gave Robert Louis Stevenson the idea to write a pirate story in the first place. On vacation in Scotland with his family, Stevenson started drawing a map one day to entertain his stepson Lloyd. Together, the two of them sketched in the features of the island and began to give the places names like Spyglass Hill and Cape of the Woods. Then they drew a line of three red crosses where they imagined buried treasure could be found. Soon they were inventing adventures and exploits that took place there. Through Stevenson's imagination were running pirates, parrots, a man with one leg,...and so began the story of *Treasure Island*.

CHAPTER FIVE

Privateers' Progress:
The Venerable Simeon Perkins

Very busy with the Prizes, Privateers, etc.

–Simeon Perkins

LIVERPOOL, NOVA SCOTIA (JULY 6, 1800)

Simeon Perkins rolled over in his bed and listened to the loud, belligerent voices of the men down on the wharf. They seemed to be fighting or arguing about something, or perhaps they were just making merry—you could never really tell with seamen. He didn't mind if they were making merry; he just wished that they wouldn't do it so very loudly and at such a very late hour when all his household was trying to sleep.

He would have been well within his rights to demand that they cease and desist—after all, he was a justice of the peace, important landowner, merchant and all around pillar of the community. But the men whose voices were currently keeping him awake were privateers in his employ. Furthermore, their brig, the *Rover*, had just sailed into harbour towing three prize ships in her wake—prize ships whose cargo might very well line the pockets of Simeon Perkins. As a part owner of the *Rover*, Perkins was entitled to a cut of the spoils, and if they sold well at auction, he would be so much the richer.

So let the men make merry or fight or argue or whatever it was they were doing, for they were the ones who brought the money home to him. Simeon Perkins turned over, closed his eyes and went back to sleep—or at least tried to.

In 1800, Liverpool was a bustling centre of trade and commerce. Every day the harbour was trafficked by merchant ships laden with the raw materials of an empire: rum, lumber, bricks, wine, brandy, flour, guns, cotton, butter, molasses, rich fabrics, corn, tar, salt, sugar, cattle, bread, herring, cod, salmon, mackerel, coffee, cocoa and huge barrels called hogsheads that could weigh 1000 pounds apiece when filled with wine or tobacco.

Liverpool had nearly 4000 citizens, a mixture of religious hard-working merchants, toughened sea-going mariners, hell-raising ne'er do wells and regular folk trying to make a living. Daily life was a contrast between refinement and rowdiness: Religious raptures occurred as regularly in church as fistfights, and dust-ups broke out in the street. People had one another over for tea or threatened each other with sticks (though rarely at the same time and rarely with the same people).

During winter, sometimes the well-to-do rode grandly through town in their horse-drawn sleighs, and other times they tore madly down the streets endangering the lives of pedestrians. One day a little boy playing with a pistol and some gunpowder blew-up the house he was in, the houses on either side and himself. Single mothers were frowned upon; black people were half-heartedly tolerated. Residents killed themselves, killed each other, lived in rude good health and died from smallpox. It was the best of times. It was the worst of times. It was Liverpool.

Simeon Perkins arrived from Connecticut in 1762 and had seen his fortunes ebb and flow with those of the town. Loyal to the English King, Perkins watched with alarm during the years of the American Revolutionary War (1776–1785) as his native land fought to tear itself away from Great Britain. When American privateers staged a raid and took over Liverpool's fort in 1780, Perkins masterminded the capture of their leaders and then convinced them to leave, all without a single death.

Although Liverpool itself was never again bothered by privateers, the war was a disaster for maritime shipping overall. Now, instead of a large and friendly market to the south, there was an enemy nation with whom trade was forbidden by English law. Furthermore, British shipping interests in North America were now under constant threat of attack from American forces.

Eight years after the Revolutionary War ended, just as things were getting back to normal, France declared war on England in 1793. Initially, things went well for England, with British forces capturing most of France's bases in the Caribbean. This gave England a huge advantage since the French now had nowhere to harbour their ships in the New World. But when Spain joined France as an ally in 1796, the situation reversed itself. Spain still had plenty of holdings in South America, and these friendly ports gave France footholds from which to launch large-scale attacks to reclaim its Caribbean holdings. With the French recapture of Guadeloupe and other islands, England was in serious trouble. Now, French privateers could prowl the waters of the Atlantic, picking off English ships as they pleased.

There was also the fledgling United States; although the U.S. had technically "won" the war and was now recognized as a sovereign nation, its economy was in a shambles and there was still widespread hostility towards recently vanquished English masters. The U.S. was an uneasy "neutral" nation between the warring factions of England, France and Spain. Canada, of course, wasn't even Canada yet; it was still a colony of Britain, and many of the "Americans," as they now called themselves, were angry at the loyalists who had refused to join the cause.

It was a frustrating time for east-coast merchant mariners both in the U.S. and British North America;

all the resources were in place to carry on a busy trade in shipping, but the opportunities were being denied. French privateers posed an increasing threat to British shipping in the New World, with fewer and fewer ships reaching Canadian maritime ports. With the bulk of the English navy tied up in Europe, there was no British presence to protect the shipping trade of its colonies. In this kind of atmosphere, turning to privateering was something of an economic necessity. Some merchants obtained letters of marque simply so they could legally carry cargo in a heavily armed ship, since one never knew when one's freight might come under attack. Others could see that for those willing to take risks, substantial profits could be made.

In the midst of his busy life as politician, militia leader, businessman, landowner, judge, privateer backer, husband and father, Simeon Perkins also found time to keep a diary. For 46 years, from 1766 to 1812, Perkins made nearly daily entries about life in Liverpool, leaving a valuable historical document of a key time in Canada's history. To a modern reader, some of the language is unintentionally hilarious: "Intercourse between England and Ireland is prohibited by proclamation." And whether he is reporting the behaviour of a deranged townsman or a minor medical problem, his style of writing is always matter of fact: "Fri. Aug 9, 1799.... Thomas Boomer gets into a Strange Phrenzey and offers to Shoot his father, and then offers to take his own life." Then a few pages later,

"I have a Sore on my little finger which threatens to be a Boil or Some bad Sore."

It is from the diary of Perkins that we gain an unusually complete picture of the privateer life-style in Canada of the late 18th and early 19th centuries. We know that he first flirted with priva-teering during the Revolutionary War, consorting with other Liverpool merchants to outfit the *Lucy* as a privateer schooner. But it wasn't until 1798 that he and other local worthies pooled their resources and built their own ship—the *Charles Mary Wentworth*, named after the son of the lieu-tenant governor of Nova Scotia, Sir John Went-worth.

DECEMBER 16, 1798

The crack of the cannon echoed across the har-bour, and then came the sound of cheering voices, once, twice, then for a third and final time. The *Charles Mary Wentworth* had returned home safe, sound and successful from her maiden voyage. Now, her privateer crew was jubilantly announc-ing their triumphant return to anyone in earshot. As the sun set they sailed the length of the river and entered the harbour, home at last.

The *Wentworth* had put to sea on her maiden voyage on August 15, and scarcely more than three weeks later, on September 10, her first prize sailed into the harbour at Liverpool. The captured ship was a Spanish brigantine, *Nostra Seignora del Car-men*, loaded with cocoa and cotton.

On November 27 another captured ship arrived, the *Morning Star*, captured north of Cuba. These two prizes brought a return of £6000, a handsome sum and a good return for a first voyage. When the *Wentworth* returned, Perkins and the other owners threw a celebratory dinner for the officers at Mrs. West's tavern. Here, they agreed to outfit the ship for a second voyage as soon as possible and also decided to combine forces with the owners of another privateer ship, the *Fly*.

On February 3, 1799, the *Fly* and the *Wentworth* set out on a new voyage, and after that, the prizes came thick and fast: on March 24 a second ship called *Nostra Seignora del Carmen* arrived in harbour, her cargo hold filled with wine, brandy and other sundries valued at over £10,000. By May 11, the *Wentworth* and four additional captures had returned. The new prize ships were three schooners, named *Casualidad, Diligence* and *Fortuna*, with the fourth being a brig named *La Liebre*. Combined with the cargo of the second *Nostra Seignora del Carmen*, the cruise had brought in about £20,000 for the privateer consortium. Their inaugural voyages had made Perkins' privateers some £26,000 richer, definitely a good return on investment.

But the business of privateering had come a long way in the last hundred years, and it was rife with risk and pitfalls. The spirit was still the same: "To distress and annoy the Trade of all His Majesty's Enemies," but gone were the days of one or two shareholders who could lay claim to the lion's share of loot. Building and outfitting a ship in 1799 was comparable to raising a skyscraper today. It required many investors, each of whom would receive a small share of any potential profits. For instance, Perkins initially owned a 1/8 share of the *Charles Mary Wentworth*, but when partnered with the *Fly*, he wound up owning a 1/16 share in both ships.

The process of converting loot into cash had also become highly regulated. If privateering at the beginning of the 1700s had been "licensed piracy," then by the 1800s it had become "piracy by bureaucracy." Once a ship had been seized and brought into port, the privateer owners had to apply to the Court of the Vice Admiralty in Halifax to see if the seized ship would be "approved" or "condemned." This process usually took about five weeks, and during that time it was forbidden to unload a captured ship's cargo unless it was in danger of being damaged. If the ship was "condemned," this was good for the privateers, since this meant that they could safely auction off the ship and all of its contents. If the ship were "approved," this was bad news—it meant that the a captain had seized a ship that had committed no wrong and the privateer backers might be required to pay a hefty fine.

In their defence, it could be extremely difficult for privateer captains to tell which ships were legitimate targets and which weren't. Captains who were worried about being boarded often carried a spare set of forged papers that falsified their ship's country of origin. When privateers came on board they would simply produce papers that showed that they came from some friendly nation. Of course, a ship with a captain who was clearly Spanish, in command of an all-French crew, with papers that said the ship was Portuguese, was probably suspect.

The problem of what actually constituted a legitimate prize was a thorny one, because the vice admiralty's rules for privateers were incredibly complicated. For instance, when French and Spanish merchants in the Caribbean realized that privateers from New Brunswick and Nova Scotia were capturing more than a few of their ships, they turned to a "neutral" nation to do their shipping—the United States of America. This made matters much more difficult—because the U.S. was a neutral nation, her ships could not be considered legal prey for privateers. This meant that a neutral ship carrying enemy property to an enemy nation could be set free if her papers and cargo were in good order.

For example, when the ship *Fabius* was sent to Liverpool by the privateer *Nymph*, even though she was carrying Spanish freight to Barcelona, the ship herself was owned by Americans. Perkins examined her papers and later wrote that he could not "See anything but what looks fair," and eventually the ship was set free with her cargo intact. Perkins and his fellow backers subsequently had to pay the *Fabius'* owners £1000 in damages.

Sometimes a cargo might be condemned while the ship itself was approved. This happened in the case of the *Morning Star.* Originally owned by British interests, the *Morning Star* had been captured by American privateers before the *Wentworth* recaptured her near Cuba. Once back in British hands, the vice admiralty ruled that although the cargo was fair game, the ship itself should be returned to her rightful owners, with Perkins' privateers receiving merely a salvage fee. It was yet another way that privateer backers might see their profits whittled away.

On top of all this, pitfalls occurred that were simply impossible to foresee. During June 1799 alone, Perkins and his partners were beset by numerous difficulties. On the 5th, the buyer of the prize ship *Casualidad* was angry that the ship had not been emptied and made ready for delivery, when in fact no date had been set for him to take possession. On the 8th, the buyer of *LaLiebre* complained that the ship's inventory included a full set of sails, which were indeed on board, but alas, they were rotten. Perkins and his fellow shareholders made it up to the buyer by allowing him to take many of the small items that had been on board when she was captured. And most painful of all, from the 13th to the 17th, as they unloaded the *Casualidad*'s cargo of cocoa (emptying it out so that its impatient new owner could take possession), they realized that their original estimate of 80 tons had been high and they really had only 54 tons, meaning a significant reduction in profit.

But through all these mix-ups, Perkins' privateers worked to enlarge their fleet and mount new expeditions. They decided to fit out one of the two captured *Nostra Seignora del Carmen*s as a privateer herself. They requisitioned 10 nine-pound guns from the government along with 4 four-pounders and renamed the ship *Duke of Kent*. For the 20 cannons already on board, they provided 20 barrels of gunpowder and threw in about one hundred cutlasses for good measure.

On June 29 the *Duke of Kent* put to sea along with the *Wentworth*, and in the coming weeks they captured four ships: the *Greyhound*, the *Josephina*, the *Lady Hammond* and the *Santo Christo del Graz*. This latter ship had about £4000 worth of cotton, cocoa and indigo on board, but the other three ships were rather disappointing by comparison, netting their captors only a few hundred pounds. Again Perkins and his shareholders set about enlarging their fleet, now converting the captured *Lady Hammond* into a privateer and renaming her the *Lord Spencer*.

By now Perkins himself owned 1/32 of the *Wentworth*, 1/16 of the *Duke of Kent* and 1/16 of the *Lord Spencer*. He also estimated that his share of the third voyage of the *Wentworth* had netted him a little more than £9, while his share in the *Duke of Kent*'s inaugural voyage probably brought in just

under £30—not much when you consider the
rewards of early voyages and the sheer amount of
work involved in administrating them.

Of course the captains and crews of Perkins' privateer vessels would probably have loved to have
such problems; while Perkins sat safely back in
Liverpool, attending to his many business interests
and worrying about money, these men put their
lives on the line every day. They survived stormy
seas and pitching oceans, knowing they might be
swept overboard at any moment; they spent hours
manning the pumps to keep their ships from sinking; they endured sickness, privation and hardship;
they invested hours or even days chasing ships
that got away; and they might spend weeks or
even months hunting the seas, but still return
empty-handed. At different times both the *Wentworth* and the *Lord Spencer* ran aground on reefs
and the *Spencer*'s crew had to abandon ship.

On one expedition, the *Wentworth* was prowling
the Spanish Main and sent a couple of landing
parties ashore to "spike" the cannons of local forts.
"Spiking" meant that the cannons were disabled
by hammering a metal spike into the opening
where a wick or fuse would normally be placed. It
gave the privateers a much greater sense of secu-
rity to know that their ships could not be destroyed
by crashing cannonballs as they approached by
sea, nor could their raiding parties be rained down
upon by fiery death.

The first attempt went well, and for June 17, 1799, the *Wentworth's* Captain, Joseph Freeman, wrote in his log:

> *Sent the boats in to Comana bay with 18 men under the Command of Lieutenant Joseph Barss to see if there was any vessels in the bay and for the purpose of Destroying a Fort that was there which mounted 18–12 and nine Pounders which they Spiked up and hove them down A High bank into the Sea. At daylight the boats returned with the Powder from the magazine and Muskets taken from the Soldiers and Spunges & rammers.*

So far so good, but on a second attempt farther down the coast, the landing party came under attack and returned fire. In the ensuing melee, Captain Freeman's cousin Nathaniel was shot and killed. Freeman wrote that his cousin had "behaved on all Expeditions Smart and Active," but there was also a lingering doubt as to whether he had been killed by an enemy bullet or by a stray bullet fired from his own forces. This lent a grim mood to the rest of the trip.

To add insult to injury, on this same voyage, the *Wentworth* appears to have fallen victim to every sailor's nightmare—impressment. "Impressment" was, in effect, abduction sanctioned by the Crown. It was a despicable practice adopted by the Royal Navy, which allowed its captains to board ships, take certain crew members by force and put them to work on their own ships. The reasoning was that the needs of the British Navy took precedence over the rights of its subjects. Impressment had been around for a long time; it was one of the factors that had led to the Golden Age of Piracy, as sailors rebelled at being forced into what amounted to slave labour in the name of their country. Impressment was also a key issue in the outbreak of the War of 1812 several years later, when U.S. sailors were routinely impressed by British ships.

As a final indignity, when the *Wentworth* sailed back into Liverpool on September 11, 40 of her crew were down with sickness, she had made no notable captures, and what prizes she had taken were lost at sea on their way back to Nova Scotia. Clearly then, being a privateer was a stressful job, both for the backers and their crews. But in spite of diminishing returns, Perkins and the other backers were already at work building another privateer ship—one that would become the most famous vessel of her kind.

SOUTH OF BERMUDA, EAST OF PORTO RICO, LAT. 23° LONG. 54° (JUNE 17, 1800)

Alex Godfrey, captain of Simeon Perkins' privateer ship *Rover*, had to make a decision and he had to make it fast. There was only one *Rover*, but there were six menacing ships bearing down on her. Godfrey knew the odds were against him and that if he took on six ships, one of which was a large and heavily armed French schooner, he would be putting the lives of his men in grave peril. Any ordinary man would have made the sensible decision to withdraw, but Godfrey was not an ordinary man, and he was certainly not an ordinary sea captain as is shown by his next action: He asked the crew what they wanted to do—and they wanted to fight!

Compared to the *Rover*'s 14 deck guns, two of the enemy ships were showing at least 16 guns each, while one of the smaller vessels was seen to carry four. Numerically, the odds were in the enemy's favour, not to mention having the advantage of greater firepower. But incredibly, when the *Rover* turned to attack, the schooner signalled the others to split up! According to an account written by Godfrey himself, "so soon as the enemy perceived our intentions, they, by signal from the schooner, dispersed, each taking a different course before we got within gunshot of them."

The intrepid crew of the *Rover* was not about to give up, however. Their veins still coursing with adrenalin from the fight they'd been denied (and probably with some relief at not being blasted to smithereens), the crew of the *Rover* gave chase. After a couple of hours, the speedier *Rover* overtook two of the runaways: an American whaler called the *Rebecca*, loaded with 1100 barrels of valuable sperm whale oil, and another American vessel, the brig *Moses Myers*, packed with wine from Madeira. Flanked by her two prizes, the *Rover* set sail for home.

At the turn of the 19th century, France and the U.S. were engaged in a sort of undeclared naval war with each other. The *Rebecca* and the *Moses Myers* were American ships that had been captured by the larger French schooner and were now captured yet again by the *Rover*. In Europe, France had also recently defeated the Dutch navy, and Holland was under French control. This worked out well for the *Rover*, because on the way back to Nova Scotia, Godfrey and his crew also captured an American sloop called the *General Greene*. The *General Greene* was carrying freight to Holland, and because Holland was now controlled by France, and since France and England were at war, and since Nova Scotia was a colony of England, the cargo of the *General Greene* was obviously bona fide "contraband." And so by this strange domino tumble of international law, Godfrey and the crew of the *Rover* had bagged what they thought was their third legitimate prize.

The *Rover* and her three prizes arrived back in Liverpool on July 4, with Simeon Perkins writing that the captured ships made "a very pritty Appearance." The usual legal wrangling followed before the ships could be disposed of, and in the end, the profits on these three prizes were rather slim, with the court approving some and condemning others. Nonetheless, Perkins and his fellow stakeholders were pleased and promptly sent the *Rover* out to sea once more.

With a fresh crew, the *Rover* set out again on July 17 and headed south once more to the shores of the Spanish Main. Looking for big Spanish merchant haulers, they lurked in the coastal shipping lanes, but to no avail. Determined to capture something, Godfrey ordered the *Rover*'s cutter (about the size of a lifeboat) to patrol the waters at night, looking for smaller prey. The tactic worked; a crewman with the unwieldy name of Lodowick Harrington commanded the little boat and conducted a series of daring nighttime raids on Spanish sloops. First their cocoa was transferred to the *Rover* and then the sloops were sunk. At one point the crew of the tiny cutter even captured a large schooner laden with salt. It is worth noting that the capture of the schooner marked the third time that Perkins' privateers had captured a ship named *Nostra Seignora del Carmen*, suggesting that Spanish mariners at the time were simply not very imaginative in naming their ships.

Between the *Rover*'s first voyage and the havoc she now wrought along the coast, the Spanish authorities had had enough of this persistent and annoying intruder. Sensing that the captain could not resist the temptation of an easy catch, the Spaniards set a trap. The Spanish governor of Port Cabello outfitted a huge schooner, the *Santa Rita*, with 125 men and various deck guns. He also outfitted three smaller gun boats with as much armament as they could bear. Then, as bait, he had a small Spanish schooner beat along the coast, where the *Rover*'s lookouts could spot her.

When he spied the apparently helpless little schooner, Godfrey gave chase and followed the ship towards the mainland where, according to Godfrey's account, he may have succeeded in sinking his quarry. But now, the three gun boats and the *Santa Rita* came out of Porto Bello harbour and sprang the trap—the *Rover* was cornered, outflanked and outgunned. Godfrey realized that he and his crew were in a dire predicament—Spain had a reputation for torturing and murdering prisoners, hence the saying, "Fall into the hands of God, not into the hands of Spain." Determined that the Spaniards would get neither the ship nor its crew, Godfrey sent his nephew below decks with a slow-burning wick. If the Spaniards should get aboard he was to touch the fuse to the powder magazine and blow up the ship.

To make matters worse, the day was a calm one—there was no wind, which made it very difficult to maneouver quickly in a fight. The Spanish had solved this problem by having two gun boats (rowed by black slaves chained to the deck) tow the schooner round the point and into the harbour. The *Rover* had no gun ships to tow her, nor slaves to row them, but she did have sweeps, long oars that could be worked from the deck of the boat to turn her at close quarters. Godfrey looked at the angle the enemy flotilla was approaching from and began to form a plan. It would require nerves of steel and split-second timing, but it was their only chance.

Godfrey let the two smaller ships move in on his port side, keeping the schooner dead astern. And now his unorthodox but brilliant plan swung into action: He ordered the oarsmen to pull hard on the port-side oars, bringing the *Rover* around in a sharp turn. The *Rover* and the schooner were now positioned at right angles to each other, in the shape of a capital "T," with the *Rover* forming the crossbar on top. From here, Godfrey unleashed all seven of his starboard guns on the schooner. For the Spanish vessel it was a disaster; her decks had been full of men ready to board the *Rover*, but now they were mown down like blades of grass, since the unusual angle of fire allowed Godfrey to hit targets fore and aft, at both ends of the schooner's decks. Now, Godfrey pulled hard on the starboard sweeps, bringing the *Rover* around so that he was more or less parallel to the two gun ships. From here he fired again, inflicting massive damage on the smaller ships. Godfrey's own account reads as follows:

> *As the enemy drew near, we engaged them with muskets and pistols, keeping with oars, the stern of the Rover toward them, and having our guns well loaded with great and small shot, ready against we should come to close quarters. When we heard the commander of the schooner give orders to the two gunboats to board us.... I then manned the oars on the larboard side and pulled the Rover around so as to bring her starboard*

*broadside to bear athwart the schooner's bow,
and poured into her a whole broadside of great
and small shot, which racked her deck fore and
aft, while it was full of men ready for boarding. I
instantly shifted over to the other side and raked
both the gunboats in the same manner, which
must have killed and wounded a great number
of those on board of them, and done great damage to their boats.*

Shipboard time was measured in "glasses," the duration it took for the sand of an hourglass to fall into its bottom, equivalent to about 30 minutes. For "three glasses" (about 90 minutes) the *Rover* and the damaged schooner exchanged broadside cannon fire until a wind finally came up. Godfrey was brave but not foolhardy; with a breeze to fill his sails, he was happy to withdraw and made ready to put out to sea. But as the *Rover* was nosing towards the open ocean, her crew heard a loud crack and looked back to see that one of the Spanish schooner's masts had collapsed. She was out of control. Godfrey saw his opportunity and seized it, bringing the *Rover* about and hastily mustering a boarding party.

When they boarded the damaged vessel, the scene was a bloodbath: out of 125 Spanish sailors and marines, 54 lay dead or wounded. The *Rover*'s crew numbered just 45, and not one of them had been injured or killed. Godfrey took a knife, cut down the Spanish flag and made ready to sail for home.

For all of Godfrey's intrepid heroics, *Rover*'s prizes only brought Simeon Perkins about £18 for his 1/32 share, though the sale of the captured ships themselves brought in better money. Always hoping for bigger and better prizes, Perkins and the other stakeholders kept sending out expeditions. They now had three ships: the *Duke of Kent*, the *Rover* and the *Nymph*. The *Charles Mary Wentworth* and the *Fly* had both been sold at auction some time ago. The remaining trio of privateers continued to put to sea and continued to bring prizes (including yet a fourth Spanish ship—named *Nostra Seignora del Carmen*!) back to Liverpool. But by 1801 peace negotiations were underway between England and France. Once there was peace, privateering would no longer be a viable way to earn money, so Perkins and his cabal of shareholders sold off their three remaining ships. When the Treaty of Amien was signed on October 1, England and France were at peace once more—but not for long.

War broke out again on May 18, 1802, and as soon as the news reached Liverpool, Perkins and the other financiers started making plans. The *Rover* had been bought by one of the *Wentworth*'s former captains, Joseph Freeman. Freeman sold the ship back to Perkins and his friends for £800, and they spent another £900 outfitting her with guns and other necessities. Unfortunately, instead of Alex Godfrey, for a captain they chose Benjamin Collins.

Benjamin Collins was simply not a good privateer captain. First, he stopped and boarded an American ship that wasn't carrying any cargo. Next, he stopped an American ship and took $1100 out of the captain's chest, claiming that even though the ship was American, the money belonged to a Frenchman. Conveniently ignoring the fact that Britain and Spain were not currently at war, he also captured a Spanish ship, the *Lanzarotte*, and sent her to Liverpool, doing the same a month later to an American ship coming home from Dutch Guiana.

In every case his actions cost his backers substantial sums instead of bringing in actual income. Two of the American ships never even made it to Liverpool, putting in at American ports and subsequently being returned to their rightful owners. As for the *Lanzarotte*, the vice admiralty court ordered Perkins' privateers not only to return the ship's cargo but also to pay an additional $1000 to her captain.

With the return of the *Rover*, Perkins seems to have called an end to his privateering activities. Perhaps he had come to feel that there was simply too little return for too much effort. Or perhaps, nearing the age of 68, he simply felt too old for all the trouble. Of the six privateers to sail from Liverpool during this time, Perkins had backed five.

Although the Napoleonic Wars kept France and England in conflict for the next 11 years, privateering dropped off somewhat after 1803. But as the first decade of the 19th century ran out, tensions were simmering once more between the U.S. and England. Badgered by Napoleon in Europe and trying desperately to hold on to her North American colonies, England's belligerence set the stage for what would be come a golden age for Canadian privateers: the War of 1812.

CHAPTER SIX

Privateers and the War of 1812

Profit is sweet, even if it comes from deception.

*–*Sophocles, Greek playwright

When the U.S. declared war on Great Britain on 18 June 1812, the American government immediately began issuing letters of marque. By August there were 150 U.S. privateers prowling the eastern seaboard. With a much smaller population, the Maritimes fielded far fewer ships, but what they lacked in numbers, they more than made up for in spirit.

AMERICAN NEWSPAPERS UP AND DOWN THE EASTERN seaboard were screaming for vengeance. A tiny clipper ship, built in Boston but now a Nova Scotia privateer, was capturing U.S. ships left, right and centre. Less than half the size of some of her victims, this persistent little vessel seemed to be everywhere at once, sometimes capturing two or three ships in a single day! As well as putting a serious dent in shipping profits, for the Americans, it was just plain embarrassing.

On December 16, 1812, *The Boston Messenger* complained, "That an insignificant fishing schooner should have captured and carried home eight or nine sail, valued at from $70,000 to $90,000, within twenty days of the time she left Liverpool, N.S. is shameful. A few weeks ago she captured within ten miles of Cape Cod, vessels with cargoes worth $50,000."

By May 1813, the *American Shipping Intelligencer* had nicknamed the little privateer, "the evil genius of our coasting trade" and went on to tell how she had eluded capture by no less than three U.S. ships, all heavily armed and equally determined. In truth, many of the claims made by the American press were somewhat exaggerated. They had alleged that the little intruder had captured 9 ships in a single battle, 11 ships in one week and 29 ships in one cruise.

But media bias of the day aside, "the evil genius" was a truly remarkable prize grabber. Between September 1812 and May 1813, she captured some 33 vessels, once bagging five ships in five days, and on another occasion, seven ships in nine days. She was devilishly fast too, taking the *Lydia* off Portland, Maine, on a Sunday and then travelling 250 miles in 24 hours under the power of sail alone to capture the *Consolation* off Martha's Vineyard on Monday. Furthermore, her commander seemed to have positively clairvoyant intuition in picking good hunting spots, always managing to turn up where the cargoes were most valuable.

Who was this maritime hunter? What was the name of his elusive little ship? How did this pint-sized marauder perform her seemingly magical feats of daring? Angry Americans were about to find out.

Off the Coast of Maine (June 11, 1813)

Joseph Barss Jr., commander of the privateer *Liverpool Packet*, must have recognized that any day his luck could run out, and this, apparently, was that day. It was never a good sign when the ship you were chasing came about and headed straight back at you, but this was precisely what happened. Now, as she drew closer, he could see that his would-be quarry was far from being a helpless merchant trader; she was actually a large and not-in-the-least-helpless American privateer. And worst of all, the day was a calm one; there was not a whisper or a breath of wind to fill his sails and help him get away.

Always cool under pressure, Barss immediately gave the order to come about. As the *Packet* headed away from the oncoming schooner, Barss considered his situation. He had a crew of only 33 men, having put the rest on captured ships to sail them home to Liverpool; the approaching American ship was almost certain to outman him. He could stay and fight, but that would be nearly suicidal; besides having smaller guns than the American, Barss also had fewer of them. And to get a clear shot he would have to stop and execute a quarter turn to take aim, a manoeuver that would allow his pursuer to gain on him. There was also the fact

that over the last 10 months his name and that of
his ship had come to be as reviled along the eastern American seaboard as they were revered in
Nova Scotia. He and his crew could not exactly
expect to be treated well if captured.

Barss came to a quick decision; if stopping and
turning to fire was not an option, then the guns
themselves were only slowing him down—overboard with them! Into the waters of the Atlantic
plunged at least four small guns, lightening the
Packet's load as they sank to the bottom of the
ocean. But one gun he kept—probably a six-
pounder. Barss ordered his men to wrestle it into
the rear cabin of the ship and to aim it out the
stern window; from here he would be able to fire
on his pursuer as he tried to get away.

For the next five hours Barss' gunners fired
their new stern gun, then reloaded it and shot
again. In the cramped and smoky confines of the
cabin, the deafening CRACK sounded in the little
room, and time and time again the gunners
stepped forward to reload. When they ran out of
six-pound balls they started wrapping four-pound
balls in canvas, stuffing them down the barrel and
hoping for luck. All the while, the larger guns of
the pursuing ship dropped shots into the water
around them, luckily missing the hull, but puncturing sails and snapping ropes.

It was obvious that the Packet would neither be
able to outgun the bigger ship, nor outrun her.

Barss took the only option left to him: he struck the ship's colours, pulling down her flag in the recognized symbol of naval surrender. The Americans were having none of it; even though the *Packet* had clearly surrendered, they leapt on to her decks with their muskets afire. The Nova Scotians shot back and at least four men on both sides were dead before the guns went quiet. The Americans took Joseph Barss prisoner, and the ship herself they took in tow, twin prizes for angry mobs in ports all along the coast.

They put ashore in Portsmouth. In blatant contravention of agreed-upon rules for the treatment of privateer captains and crews, Barss and his men were paraded through the town in chains. Crowds lined the streets to see these privateers who had wrought such havoc on their ships. Jeers, taunts and yells followed them along the muddy streets until finally they reached the old jail on Islington Street. And there at last, after hours of deafening cannon fire and miles of screaming mobs, Joseph Barss found quiet—as the door of his prison cell slammed shut behind him.

Joseph Barss was, of course, not an "evil genius," nor did he have clairvoyant powers.

He was a Nova Scotian born in Liverpool in 1776. His father, Joseph Barss Sr., was a well-respected sea captain and acquaintance of Simeon Perkins. As the son of a prominent mariner, Barss Jr. could expect to follow in his father's footsteps, and at the age of 14 he went to work on one of Barss Sr.'s fishing vessels. At that time Liverpool's seafaring folk formed an inner circle of long-standing professional relationships and personal friendships. Family members and business interests intermarried easily, and by the time he was 22 Barss Jr. was second lieutenant on the *Charles Mary Wentworth*, one of the privateer ships backed by his father's friend Simeon Perkins. The next year he was made captain of the smaller privateer *Lord Spencer* but got off to an inauspicious start by running her aground on a reef. He also briefly commanded the famous *Rover*, faring a bit better and managing to capture three ships.

His early voyages as a captain may not have been particularly profitable, but they gave him valuable experience in the ways of privateering. He learned the trade routes most favoured by merchant captains and became familiar with the layout of the eastern seaboard. He plotted the location of every bay, inlet and harbour. The rise and fall of the wind became as natural to him as his own breath. Likewise, the years spent on his father's fishing boats gave him a wide knowledge of sailing lore. He knew what captains looked for when they tried to identify a ship that was no more than a speck on the horizon. The shape of her sails, the angle of her masts and they way she sat in the water—all of these things he put into practice every day. And though he couldn't have known it at the time, this palette of experience, knowledge and insight meant that 200 years later, people would still be writing books about him.

When the U.S. declared war on Britain on June 18, 1812, Britain herself was slow to follow suit, not returning the favour until October 13. This meant that in the intervening months there was no legitimate mechanism for the issuing of letters of marque against American vessels. The aspiring privateers of Newfoundland, Nova Scotia and New Brunswick would have to wait. But waiting was the one thing they could not afford to do. For one thing, there was money to be made, and for another, the U.S. privateers were busily attacking British and Canadian interests wherever and whenever they could.

Nova Scotia Lieutenant Governor Sir John Sherbrooke (later to have not one but two privateer vessels named after him) took it upon himself to issue letters of marque under his own authority, without waiting for approval from England. The legitimacy of these papers depended on a loophole in their wording; Mother England may not yet have been at war with the U.S., but she was definitely at war with France. Even though there was nary a Frenchman in sight (with all of France's navy being tied up in Europe), the owners of the *Packet* applied for, and received, letters of marque "against France, &c" ("&c" was short for "etcetera"). Knowing that the Court of the Vice Admiralty would be on their side, the *Packet*'s owners interpreted "etcetera" to mean that they could attack England's enemies as they saw fit—and that is exactly what they did.

The *Packet* first sailed as a privateer on August 31, 1812. On September 7 she was just off Georges Bank, the fertile fishing grounds just east of Maine and south of Nova Scotia. The banks were named for St. George, patron saint of England, and appropriately enough, the *Packet* was about to strike a blow for England. The *Middlesex* was a large U.S. ship bound for New York, and no sooner had the *Packet* caught sight of it than she was stopped and boarded. But as soon as Barss' boarding party set foot on her decks, the captain of the *Middlesex* produced a British licence giving him permission to carry freight between England and the U.S. So instead of enjoying a nice, simple capture, the *Packet* was now tangled up in a dense knot of red tape—a knot trailing back to the very causes of the War of 1812.

One reason for the U.S. declaration of war had been Britain's so-called Orders in Council. Since England was at war with France, the Orders in Council authorized British ships to blockade French seaports. It was economic warfare and it worked; England had effectively cut off the flow of overseas supplies to France. As a result, neutral nations that had no quarrel with either France or England were forced to trade only at English ports, since any ship attempting to sail into a French port would be fired upon by the blockading English.

The U.S. was one such neutral nation. Frustrated, but not thinking clearly, the U.S. government retaliated with the senseless Embargo Act, which forbade American ships from docking at any foreign port. When this had no effect on either England or France, the U.S. government went one better and pushed through the prudish-sounding Non-Intercourse Act. The Act stipulated that, on second thought, American ships could sail into any foreign port—except Britain or France. It was like cutting off your own leg and then shooting the severed limb in the foot for good measure.

For the sea-going merchants of the eastern American seaboard, these laws were ruinous. They had spent long years and vast sums of money building an industry, but were now denied the chance to practise it. Some American merchants refused to stop trading with Britain and secretly applied to the English authorities for special licences that would grant them safe passage if intercepted by English ships...or colonial privateers. It was just such a licence as this that the captain of the *Middlesex* produced, and here is where the story of the *Liverpool Packet* picks up again.

SEPTEMBER 7, 1812

Joseph Barss Jr. took one look at the impressive-looking document that the captain of the *Middlesex* was holding out to him and promptly decided to ignore it. Was the captain not aware that a state of war now existed between their two nations? As a matter of fact, no, the captain wasn't aware of this, since he had been at sea when war was declared, and this was the first he had heard of it. No matter, replied Captain Barss, the *Middlesex* and her cargo were to be impounded forthwith as spoils of war. They would now be sailed home by a prize crew from the *Packet*.

No sooner was the prize master of the *Packet* installed as commander of the *Middlesex* than another speck of sail appeared on the horizon. It proved to be the *Factor*, an American ship carrying a load of Portuguese wine home to Rhode Island. The *Factor* was not having a good voyage; on August 20 she had been boarded and looted by English privateers, who took a large quantity of silver and drank a good portion of her wine. Now, for the second time in less than a month she was boarded by privateers who proceeded to drink the rest of the wine and probably would have taken the silver if there had been any left. The *Packet* headed back to Liverpool with her brace of prizes in tow.

As it turned out, Barss had bungled badly on his first outing. To begin with, the vice admiralty court upheld the licence of the *Middlesex*, ruling that it had been obtained in good faith and was still valid even though war had broken out in the meantime. The ship and her cargo were sent home to their owner in New York. The *Factor*, meanwhile, was an American ship en route to an American port,

but her cargo was the property of a neutral nation—
Portugal. The last of the wine went back to its rightful owners, while the ship itself was deemed fair
game and sold at auction.

Of course, all this took months to sort out. On
September 13, when he sailed triumphantly into
Liverpool's harbour with his two prizes in tow,
Barss had no reason to feel anything but proud.
Once the captured ships had been safely anchored
and duly reported, he lost no time in turning
around and putting to sea once more.

The *Liverpool Packet* was a remarkable vessel. She
had been built in Boston and was christened the
Black Joke. Under this name, she started her career
sailing alongside large slave ships, carrying supplies. In 1811, she was bought at auction in Halifax
by Enos Collins, one of Liverpool's most venerable
mariners. Collins had been first mate on the
Charles Mary Wentworth and was no stranger to privateering.

Renamed and refitted, the little schooner was
rather an odd sight. Her masts slanted backwards
at a steeper angle than most other ships—this gave
her a pointed, aggressive appearance as she skipped
across the waves. Her bowsprit was rigged with
three big "head" sails for extra speed. Then there
was her size—she was only 53 feet long, not quite
19 feet across and weighed in at 67 tons. By comparison, her first prize, the *Middlesex*, weighed
325 tons and would have been well over 100 feet

long, more than twice the length of the *Packet*. For her diminutive stature, she was also heavily armed; guns firing four-pound shot would have been the norm for a ship her size, but the *Packet* also packed several six-pounders and one or two 12-pounders as well.

The *Packet*'s second cruise wasn't particularly successful. The only ship she captured was the *Maria*, a Spanish vessel sailing under a prize crew of American privateers who had just taken her. Now she was captured again by Barss' crew and escorted home to Nova Scotia. But on his third cruise immediately following, Barss truly hit his stride, taking five ships in five days: the *Polly*, the *Union*, the *Four Brothers*, the *Little Joe* and a fifth ship whose name is unknown—possibly she contained no cargo and was released. But the cargoes of the other four yielded a profitable haul of rice, cotton, leather, shoes, gin, peppers, hops, fish oil, sugar, lumber, corn, flour, salt, vinegar, cheese and...bonnets.

On his fourth cruise, Barss equalled the record set on his third, capturing a ship a day for five days straight: on November 10 it was the *Edward and Hiram*; on the 11th, the *New Forge*; on November 12, the *Lucretia*; on the 13th, the *Julian*; and on the 18th, the brigantine *Economy* fell to the little privateer from Liverpool.

With a record like this, it's no wonder that U.S. newspapers began reporting exaggerated tales of

Barss' successes. In all fairness, he certainly captured and boarded many more ships than he deliv-
ered back to Liverpool. Many of them he released,
either because their cargoes were not profitable, or
because he simply didn't have any men left to sail
them, with all of his prize crews already taking
captured vessels home to Canada. The one question on everyone's lips was, how was he doing it?

There was no great mystery about Barss' success—it was all down to good seamanship, innate
cunning and the will to dare the odds. To start
with, Barss' years of service at sea before becoming
a privateer were of enormous value—he knew how
to sail a ship and how to sail it well. He also took
advantage of knowledge common to any seafaring
man worth his salt. For instance, the *Packet* came
from the shipyards in Boston and her makers had
built her with lines and rigging that, to a practiced
eye, were obviously those of an American ship.
Conveniently for Barss, his prey was…American
ships. U.S. captains on seeing this harmless-look-
ing little schooner would assume she was on their
side and would have little hesitation in approaching. It also meant that U.S. privateers, seeing her
from a distance, would assume she posed no threat
and so might be less likely to investigate.

Barss also seems to have been a crafty as a fox.
Knowing that the distinctive backward slant of the
Packet's masts would identify his ship even at a distance, he added extra topsails to confuse the eyes
of enemy captains. It was fairly common practice

in those days to add extra topsails for speed, but Barss' use of this method was almost certainly for camouflage as well. He also carried a full set of waist cloths for the *Packet*. Waistcloths were huge sheets of fabric that could be draped around a ship lengthways. They were sometimes used as ceremonial decorations, but privateers also used them to disguise their true strength by covering the ports that cannons stuck out of. They also hid the gunners from sharpshooters on rival ships. If one encountered a ship in waistcloths at sea, she was either trying to hide her impressive weaponry or disguise the fact that she didn't have any.

To further add to the confusion, many American mariners had seen the ship quite often when she was still the *Black Joke* and did not realize that her name had been changed. The first mate of the *Economy* solemnly swore in court that his ship had been captured by the privateer called "the Black Joke...commanded by Joseph Bates." Either the ship's former captain had been named Bates—or Barss had simply lied about his name. Whether by design, accident or fate, Joseph Barss appears to have had a natural flair for the art of deception.

He also seems to have possessed boundless confidence in his ship, his crew and his own judgment, going up against larger and more heavily armed ships on a daily basis. With an apparent zest for risk and an appetite for conquest, Barss was a born leader. But tempering all this was the serious demeanour of a seasoned mariner who had seen first-hand the dangers of life at sea. He had weathered more than his fair share of violent seas and foul skies. He also knew the pitfalls of privateering. As a young man Barss had served on the *Charles Mary Wentworth* and had seen one of his fellow crewmen die from a stray gunshot during a raiding expedition in South America. But as daring as Joseph Barss was, he was no foolhardy swashbuckler.

In comparison to her earlier outings, the *Liverpool Packet*'s fifth cruise was fairly routine, with a mere four ships captured: the *Three Friends*, the *Eliza*, the *Susan* and the *Colombia*. When the *Packet* sailed home though, her previous captures were still moored in the harbour for everyone to see— and with the four most recent prizes, there were now 21 of them. Her sixth cruise began in February 1813 with Barss and his crew chalking up a perfectly respectable tally of seven captures in nine days. It is also worth pointing out that three of these ships—the *Bunker Hill*, the *Reliance*, and the *Hero*—were all captured in one day.

It is difficult to accurately assess Barss' tally of captures during the time he commanded the *Packet*, but an estimate of about 100 seems fair. Thirty-three of these made it home to Liverpool, with American papers always reporting that many more had been stopped and boarded if not actually taken. In some cases Barss certainly boarded ships and then released them, but the U.S. papers were far from editorially neutral. Sometimes they deliberately set out to drive public opinion, and even though they may not have made up stories wholesale, neither did they bother to check their facts too closely. They had every interest in whipping up patriotic fervour with exaggerated tales of the "evil genius" because nothing sells papers like a witch hunt. Even before Barss' capture, the seagoing folk of Salem, Massachusetts (a community that knew a thing or two about witch hunts), had mounted the maritime equivalent of a lynch mob to track down the *Packet*.

On November 12, 1812, Captain James McCarthy stalked through the streets of Salem waving an American flag, followed by a second man beating a drum and a third playing a fife. By the time they reached the waterfront, the mob had grown to 70, at which point they boarded a ship provided by local merchants, the *Helen*. They set about modifying her to carry guns, and at nine that night this vengeful crew cast off from the docks and— just sat there, because there was no wind.

When daylight broke the next day, they were still in sight of the harbour. This pretty much set the tone for the whole cruise, and a few days out they met a sloopful of men from one of the ships that had been capured by Barss. The men told McCarthy that Barss had mentioned he was heading for St. John, New Brunswick. Not so brave as to sail into hostile waters, the *Helen* turned around and sailed back to Salem. If she had kept hunting though, she probably would have found the *Packet* lurking just off the coast. The tale about sailing to St. John was just that—a tale told by Barss to deliberately misinform anyone who questioned his former captives too closely.

After his capture in 1813, Joseph Barss Jr. spent months languishing in his cell. The men he commanded had long since been released, but the "evil genius" himself was far too dangerous a man to set free. When at last he was let go, his American captors forced him to sign a document swearing that he would never again take up arms as a privateer against the U.S. However, there are reports that he was captured again and imprisoned a second time, suggesting that Barss may have been unable to resist the excitement of commanding a privateer and sailed into battle once more.

In the end though, privateering was good to Barss. When the *Packet* first sailed, he was just a commander, but by the time of his fourth cruise he had been promoted to full captain. When he was finally done with American prisons, he took his privateer's payout and bought a farm in Kentville in 1817. There, he fathered a vast family and died at the age of 47.

Even though Barss' career on the *Packet* ended with his capture, the vessel herself continued sailing. The Americans renamed her *Young Teazer's Ghost* and sent her out as a privateer, whereupon she captured a single prize and was put up for auction. Her new owners renamed her the *Portsmouth Packet* and sent her out to plunder the seas, but before she could do any plundering a British warship captured her and she was put up for auction once more. At this point she was bought again by—who else—Enos Collins, her former owner. He renamed her the *Liverpool Packet* and found a new captain named Caleb Seely. Although Seely was no Joseph Barss, he did manage to capture 14 ships in 11 months. When Seely took his earnings and bought his own ship, the *Packet*'s command was given over to another Liverpudlian, Lewis Knaut. By this time though, England realized that it had to lend some sort of naval support to its North American colonies. Now, as well as France, Britain blockaded the American seaboard and there were fewer ships to capture. Sadly for Knaut, he only took four ships.

As for the money from the 11 months of Joseph Barss' captaincy, it took until 1814 for the vice admiralty courts to fully settle up. In the meantime, Enos Collins built a huge warehouse in Halifax to store all the loot while the lawyers hashed it out. By the time the *Packet*'s spoils were duly sold at auction, the gross was £27,019. Out of that, court fees and lawyers ate up £5000, leaving about £22,000. Of this Collins and the other backers took about £11,000, with the other half going to the crew. As commander and later captain, Barss probably got about £1000 of this money, with the other £10,000 being divided up among the *Packet*'s various crew members (sometimes she had been outfitted with entirely new crews when putting in at Liverpool), with each man probably receiving about £156.

But whatever the payout, the devastating effect on American shipping interests was undeniable. With 86 confirmed prizes put up for auction, the wrath of the U.S. merchants was understandable. At one point, outraged politicians even investigated building a canal across Cape Cod so that they would no longer need to transport their wares in vulnerable ships.

After the war, the sturdy little *Packet* was sold to new owners in Jamaica, and after that the ship's fate is a mystery. We do not know whether she spent her last days at sea, lost in a blustering gale, or ended up ashore, rotting in dry-dock. Or maybe she was simply traded from owner to owner until her ribs began to sag and her boards to warp. But whatever her end may have been, the *Liverpool Packet* lives on in memory as a symbol of Canadian defiance and triumph.

The Red Jack

The Royal Navy jealously guarded its status as Britain's defender on the seas. It was forbidden for privateer vessels to fly flags, pendants or any other insignia that might cause them to be identified as official military vessels. So, in 1740, articles were drafted that required privateer ships to fly "a red jack, with the Union Jack" in the upper corner nearest the flag staff. And for the next 80 years, a "red jack" flying from ship's bowsprit was the equivalent of a bumper sticker stating "Privateers On Board."

CHAPTER SEVEN

The *Dart*

Vessels large may venture more,
But little boats should keep near shore.

          –Benjamin Franklin

THE *LIVERPOOL PACKET* WAS NOT THE ONLY PRIVATEER AFIELD during the War of 1812. In addition to the *Packet*, Nova Scotia also mustered many others, including the *Retaliation*, the *Retrieve*, the *Wolverine*, the *Snapdragon*, the *Rolla*, the *Minerva*, the *Crown*, the *Fly*, the *Gleaner*, the *Shannon*, the *Intrepid* and the *Lunenberg*.

New Brunswick put forth the *General Smyth*, the *Brunswicker*, the *Hunter* and, most famously, the *Dart*. The *Dart* is well known to us because the logs and papers from one of her cruises have been preserved largely intact. They open a rare window into the adventures and daily life of this intrepid little privateer. But in stark comparison to the glowing resumé of the *Liverpool Packet*, these records serve to underline the confusing and often futile lot that was the life of a privateer.

Just off the Coast of Maine (May 29, 1813 – 2:30 am)

To Captain John Harris of the privateer *Dart*, it felt as though the earth had suddenly shaken beneath his feet. The problem was that he wasn't anywhere near solid land; he was standing on the deck of his ship peering into the soupy darkness of a foggy Atlantic night. Just a moment before, he had heard a pair of dull thuds, like twin cannon shots muffled by fog, which was precisely what they were. And a moment before *that*, someone had seen a pair of ghostly sails loom out of the swirling fog and vanish again. They had just been fired on by a spectral ship whose cannonballs were anything but ghostly. A moment later, one of the crew hurriedly scrambled up from below decks, reporting that there was a cannonball in his bunk and that water was pouring in through a hole below the waterline.

Harris cursed under his breath; he had fallen in alongside the British warship *HMS Rattler* because he had hoped her bulk and armament would discourage any would-be attackers. But then the fog had set in and the ships had lost sight of one another, and now it looked as if his hopes had been in vain. Then there was a commotion at one of the rails and somebody clambered aboard the *Dart* from a small boarding boat. It could only be someone from the vessel that had fired on them. Were they being boarded by enemy privateers?

To Harris' surprise, the man who had just come aboard identified himself as a crewman of...the *HMS Rattler*. When the *Rattler*'s lookout had seen the *Dart*'s sails in the fog, he had mistaken her for an American ship, and Captain Gordon had given the order to fire and...well, they were sorry about that, but after all, the Americans had a reputation for shooting first and asking questions later. Captain Gordon was only following suit, and they would send the *Rattler*'s carpenter on board just as soon as they could, to repair the damage. A few minutes later, the carpenter arrived and patched the hole as best he could, which wasn't really very well at all since the hole was below the waterline. When the carpenter was done, the *Dart* limped off into the leaden light of the grey dawn, taking on water whenever her bow dipped below the waves.

Finally, Harris found a safe place to anchor and had his crew transfer water barrels, ammunition and guns to the ship's stern. With all the weight in her stern, the *Dart*'s bow rose up out of the water enough that the hole from the cannonball was well above the surface of the water. Now her carpenter could set about repairing the wound in her side.

Like the *Liverpool Packet*, the *Dart* was a comparatively little vessel, but whereas the *Packet* was a two-masted schooner, the *Dart* was a single-masted sloop. Weighing 47 tons and measuring just 60 feet from bow to stern, at her widest point the *Dart* was a mere 18 feet across. She was armed with four carronades—short, fat cannons produced by the Carron ironworks in Scotland. A carronade was designed to fire a ball like a regular cannon, but its short barrel length reduced the velocity of the ball, which resulted in more flying splinters when it smashed into the wooden hull of a ship. More flying splinters meant more injured men, and so this was generally seen as a good thing.

In addition to the carronades, the *Dart* also carried swivel guns. As their name suggests, swivel guns could be turned and tilted. With a barrel length of about 3 feet, they looked like miniature cannons. They were not ship smashers, but rather anti-personnel weapons, and would have been packed with grapeshot or canister shot designed to spread out over a wide area to shatter bones and butcher flesh. They could also be aimed upwards to shred enemy sail canvas. The big advantage of swivel guns was that they were small enough to be moved around easily and could be bolted to a ship's rail or deck with comparative ease.

The *Dart*'s small size meant that she could only hold enough supplies and equipment to cruise for about three weeks. After that she would have to put back into shore for fresh goods or commandeer (steal) them from other vessels. Seemingly, in cases like this, Captain Harris tried to be fair, writing at one point in his log, "Went on board a Boat and got some fresh fish, for which I gave them A Bottle of Rum." But on other occasions, Harris seems to have just taken what he wanted, writing that the *Dart* had stopped and boarded a ship only to find that most interesting items in the hold were "a cargo of potatoes and one barrel of pork. Released her after taking the barrel of pork and some potatoes." Another time, the crew had rowed ashore to investigate a beached ship and came back with three barrels of sea biscuits they had discovered on board. Seemingly the captain of the *Dart* was never one to turn down a free meal.

According to the *Dart*'s Articles of Agreement, profit from the sale of seized goods would be divided between her crew of 45: the commander got eight shares; first lieutenants each got five; the four prize masters (who were authorized to take command of captured ships and sail them home) got four shares apiece; and the bosun, purser, carpenter and both gunners were entitled to three shares each. And after that the shares dribbled away into double shares, shares and a half, single shares and even three-quarter shares for the likes of the ship's boys. There was also an incentive program of sorts: The man who first spied the sail of an eventual prize received just over £1, and the first man to actually board a prize would get £5 for bravery.

But for any of this to work, the *Dart* had to actually capture prizes, and that proved to be difficult. Before getting in the way of the *Rattler*'s friendly fire, the *Dart* had been out for five weeks and had only stopped one potential prize. The *Sally* was a little schooner boarded by First Lieutenant Mr. Ross, but since she was found to have a British licence and also no cargo, she was let go, and the *Dart* sailed on.

Even after the hole in her bow was properly mended, the *Dart*'s pickings were slim. Part of the problem was that the very success of British colonial privateering meant that American ships were being much more cautious about where and when they put to sea. Therefore, the pickings close to shore were mainly smaller craft, like "Chebacco" boats.

Chebacco boats were little double-masted vessels about 40–50 feet long. They had originated in the parish of Chebacco (now Essex), Massachusetts. Since coastal towns in North America had an ample supply of fish on their doorstep, they had no need of huge fishing boats to haul in tons and tons at a time. They could send out smaller vessels to supply local needs as required. Chebacco boats were the answer. Round bodied with a pleasantly plump appearance, they were soon plying their fishy trade in great numbers.

Letters of marque for most British privateers during the War of 1812 forbade them from stopping fishing boats, since it was generally recognized that fishermen, no matter whose "side" they were on, were simply trying to earn an honest living. Privateers were strictly "required not to take, interrupt, or detain any ship or vessel which may be furnished with a British license and to abstain from all Predatory Acts…upon any unarmed Fishing Vessel peaceable following said Fishery." Captain Harris of the *Dart* once wrote in his log that upon sighting a 60-ton fishing schooner out of Boston, she was released "in view of her calling."

Perhaps this was why he gave a bottle of rum to the vessel he took fresh fish from later in his cruise.

The *Dart*'s cruise was a frustrating mixture of failure coupled with the odd success. The schooner, *Union,* was boarded but released since she wasn't carrying any cargo. Another pursuit yielded only the sea biscuits already mentioned, while on a different occasion *Dart* gave chase to an errant Chebacco boat, only to have her get away.

Finally though, on June 1, the *Dart*'s luck changed: They captured a ship that actually had cargo in her hold. The *Joanna* was a little schooner from Martha's Vineyard, and she was pulling for Halifax, loaded with 1500 bushels of corn belonging to the captain, one Alex Newcombe. Captain Newcombe was actually sailing under a British licence, but when he spotted the *Dart*, he mistook her for an American privateer and so wasn't about to produce a piece of paper that would prove he was colluding with the enemy.

However, once he realized that the *Dart* was a Canadian privateer, he hastily pulled out his licence. Captain Harris was having none of it, however. He told Newcombe that the licence was worth nothing, and that the *Joanna*'s cargo was hereby seized in the name of the Crown. Captain Newcombe objected strenuously and insisted that he be taken to St. John with his ship. Again Harris refused, writing in the log: "Put Nathanial Ricker,

prize-master, and three hands on board ye *Joanna*
and ordered her for St. John. Allowed the master
to go on shore in his boat. He wished to continue
in ye Prize, but he made use of such threatening
language that it was thought prudent to send him
ashore."

In Newcombe's later statement to the court, he
swore that Harris had threatened that "if he did
not pull away from the Privateer he would sink
the Boat in which he was." Seemingly then, Newcombe was put overboard in the *Joanna*'s cutter,
but refused to sail ashore, clinging to his ship and
hurling insults and hollow threats at her captors.
Weary of the tirade, Harris appears to have threatened to blow him out of the water. Surprisingly,
the vice admiralty court in Halifax sided with Harris and awarded claim on the *Joanna* and her cargo
to the *Dart*'s backers. Of course, things might have
gone differently if Captain Newcombe and his
licence had been allowed to actually appear in
court, instead of being put ashore in Maine.

Then on June 5, after an on-again off-again
chase that lasted most of the day, the *Dart* caught
two American ships travelling together. One was a
little Chebacco boat, the *Superb*, with her bow
painted bright red and carrying a cargo of salt. The
other was a brand new schooner, the *Washington*,
whose hull already had a row of ports for cannons
cut into it, but as yet had no guns. Harris deduced
that her owners intended to outfit her as a privateer. In the log, he wrote, "Ye schooner proved to

be ye *Washington* of Portland…a beautiful pilot boat of 65 tons, entirely new, pierced for guns, completely fitted, and I expect, was intended for a Privateer."

Now, Harris had prisoners from three captured vessels to contend with: those from the *Joanna*, the *Superb* and the *Washington*. He loaded them all onto the *Superb* and set them free along with her cargo of salt. They were close to Boston, and the sailors from the bigger vessels would have no trouble piloting the little Chebacco boat into port. Then Harris set his men to mounting swivel guns on the rails of the *Washington* before they sailed her back home. The *Dart*'s letters of marque applied not only to the *Dart* herself, but also to any ships she captured. This was fairly common practice for the time—prize vessels could be converted into privateers without the tedious necessity of returning to port to apply for new letters of marque. It allowed enterprising privateer captains to build up a little fleet that would be completely legal for the duration of the cruise. In the case of the *Washington* though, the new guns were being added more for self-defence on the way home than with any intent of capturing more ships.

The next day, on June 6, the *Dart* zigzagged back and forth for five hours and fired two shots before finally taking the *Cuba*, a 176-ton vessel loaded with flour. The *Cuba*'s captain quickly produced a licence signed by Nova Scotia Lieutenant Governor Sir John Sherbrooke that permitted him to import flour from New York to Halifax. U.S. ships carrying

U.S. cargoes and heading for U.S. ports were fair game for privateers, but not if they were travelling to Canada under a British licence.

Since trading with the enemy was forbidden, devious U.S. captains secretly obtained licences from Canada and then claimed they were heading for an American port in a more or less northeasterly direction. Of course, once cleared by U.S. port inspectors, they would continue north into Canadian waters. But Captain Harris knew that it was a common ploy for American merchants to obtain such licences, then deliver their cargo to other American ports instead of Canada. He didn't believe the complicated web of half-truths spun by the *Cuba*'s captain and sailed the captured ship back to St. John.

Here again, the *Dart*'s luck held, and the trade court took a dim view of the *Cuba*'s tactics. Her log book, produced in evidence, said clearly that she was headed for New Haven, but this was probably for the benefit of a customs inspector in New York. As the crew of the *Dart* pointed out, when they captured the *Cuba*, she was heading not for New Haven but for Portland, though her captain claimed he was really pulling for Nova Scotia. In sworn affidavits, the *Cuba*'s crew only confirmed this web of deception: One crewman reported that he had been told they were heading for Portland plain and simple; the man who had been steering when the *Cuba* was captured said he had no idea where the ship was bound; a seaman said that

Portland had definitely been their destination; the cook had no idea where the ship was going; and finally there was the crewman who freely admitted that the *Cuba*'s destination was unknown to him because, on the day she sailed, he had just gotten out of jail. Faced with so many conflicting stories, the vice admiralty awarded the prize to the owners of the *Dart*.

The *Dart*'s cruise under Harris ended on June 30, but she soon set sail again with her former first lieutenant, James Ross, as captain. Ross seems to have fancied himself more of a pirate than a privateer. In one instance he boarded a merchant ship, the *Governor Strong*, threatened the captain and crew at gunpoint, stole $500 and went on his way. Daring and lawless as he was, however, Ross' days as a pirate captain were numbered. After his blatantly illegal piracy aboard the *Governor Strong*, the U.S. Revenue Cutter *Vigilant* was dispatched to track down the errant privateer. The *Vigilant* was a big ship, with four 12-pounders, two long-barrelled six-pounders and six swivel guns. In the ensuing fire fight, the *Vigilant* was able to stay out of the range of the *Dart*'s little carronades, all the while pummelling her with larger guns.

When the crew of the *Vigilant* went aboard, they found that one of their cannonballs had killed the *Dart*'s first lieutenant, cutting him messily in half at the waist. The *Dart*'s crew all begged for mercy and fled below decks rather than put up a fight. Captain Ross, however, emerged from his cabin, seized a musket and shot a sentry in the arm—dishonourable conduct indeed from a man whose crew had just surrendered! Furthermore, he denied taking any money from the *Governor Strong*, whereupon the boarding party forced open his strong box to find—lo and behold—$500. Ross was taken into custody and, along with the *Dart*, sailed off to Portland.

Between June 1812, when the war was just getting under way, and May 1815, when the last cases dribbled through the courts, the vice admiralty in Halifax heard no fewer than 600 cases involving prize claims. As the war drew into its second year though, the British navy set up a blockade on the eastern coast of the U.S. It proved to be incredibly effective, and privateers soon found that U.S. ships were few and far between. What ones there were became much more canny and cautious in their routes and their tactics. For ambitious privateers, the waters of the eastern seaboard were not as profitable as they once had been, and with the end of the war, the golden age of Canadian privateering came to a close.

War of 1812
Privateer Vessels with Amusing Names

Halifax Bob

Lively

Weazel

Thinks I to Myself

Saucy Sixteen

CHAPTER EIGHT

Cutthroat Chronicles

In the case of pirates, say, I would like to know whether that profession of theirs has any peculiar glory about it. It sometimes ends in uncommon elevation, indeed; but only at the gallows.

–Herman Melville, author of *Moby Dick*

GRUESOME, VIOLENT MURDER IS ONE ASPECT OF PIRACY THAT many pirate fanciers tend to overlook. After all, which image is more appealing: a jolly rascal with a parrot on his shoulder, merrily bellowing, "Yo-ho-ho," or a group of sadistic men who gang-rape women, break their backs and throw them overboard? The following chapters will make disturbing reading for some. The pirates described herein are neither jolly, nor likeable. They are violent, murderous and wantonly cruel. Their tales come to us through the court transcripts of their trials, often with graphically vivid descriptions of the horrors perpetrated by the accused. Some of these wretched souls were tried not only for crimes of piracy but also for murdering their fellow pirates in the course of mutinies and shipboard conflicts. There are also heart-rending tales of dashed hopes for better lives, trusting natures taken advantage of and marital trusts betrayed.

Before he turned to piracy, John Phillips was an honest tradesman. Born into a family of shipwrights in England, he followed in the steps of his forebears and became a carpenter. He soon heard that far off Newfoundland was a bustling maritime hub with a big demand for ships' carpenters. Dreaming of a more prosperous life, Phillips set sail for the New World in 1720. Unfortunately, en route, the ship he was travelling on was captured by Thomas Anstis.

Anstis had begun his piratical career under captain Howell Davis. After Davis was killed in a raiding operation, Anstis hoped to win the command for himself. But his hopes were dashed when the rest of the pirate crew elected Bartholomew Roberts as their new captain. When Roberts' ship, the *Good Fortune*, was subsequently stolen out from under him by his own pirates, the ringleader had been none other than Thomas Anstis.

Because he was a carpenter, upon his capture by Anstis, Phillips was immediately impressed into the pirate crew. Carpenters were a valued commodity in the pirating world since ships were always in need of repair, especially after being blown half to pieces in battle. In most cases, carpenters on captured ships could expect to be forced into service whether they wanted to be pirates or not.

Phillips though, seems to have served somewhat willingly, since he signed the pirates' Articles of Agreement soon after his capture.

By the 1720s, fantastic tales of piratical exploits had sailed into the public's imagination. English taverns rang with the envious voices of regular folk wishfully gossiping about lives more deliciously wicked than theirs could ever hope to be—lifestyles of the rich and infamous. Pirates like Blackbeard, Edward Low and Bartholomew Roberts were all reputed to have amassed huge fortunes of plundered riches. They went where they pleased, did as they wanted and thumbed their noses at authority. For poor, honest landlubbers, the lure of piracy was obvious—opulent wealth, high adventure and a life as far from poverty and tedium as the imagination could conjure. In another few years a book entitled *The General History of Pyrates,* by Captain Johnson, would become a runaway bestseller. The public's misguided fascination with these rogues of the sea had begun.

It is quite possible that Phillips regarded his capture by Anstis as a piece of good fortune. Dreams of a life less ordinary may have led him to sign the Articles of Agreement wholeheartedly. Or he may have simply decided that if he had to serve, he might as well get a cut of the profits. Either way, Phillips was soon witness to a horrifying spectacle that must surely have banished any ideas of romance lurking in his head.

Off Martinique, Anstis' little pirate fleet captured a ship called the *Irwin*. One of the female passengers was subsequently raped by 20 of the pirates, who also beat the *Irwin's* captain to a bloody pulp when he tried to intervene. Either during the rape or after, the woman's back was broken and she was thrown overboard to drown. Standing by while this crime of animal brutality unfolded in front of him strongly affected Phillips (we can only assume that he did not take part). When he became a pirate captain in his own right, he drew up Articles of Agreement that meted out harsh penalties to any pirate assaulting a female captive.

Anstis' pirates decided to pre-emptively seek a collective pardon and drew up a so-called round robin petition for clemency. "Round robin" referred to a practice in which each pirate signed his name as part of a circle of signatures. On regular documents pertaining to ship's business, the captain, commander and officers signed their names at the top of the crew list. But requests for pardons were different; if they were rejected, the Crown might try to pin most of the blame on the officers. This meant that even if all the crew members swore equal responsibility, the men whose names were at the top of the list might take more of the blame. The petitions were meant to hinder the courts in assigning more blame to any one individual. Since no man's name was at the top, prosecutors would not be able to tell who the ringleaders were.

What happened next is unclear. According to
some accounts, the pardon was granted, but others
say it was denied. What is known is that Phillips
wound up back in England living with friends in
Devonshire. Soon though, he went to Topsham
and set sail once more for Canada. This time he
actually made it.

Settling in Newfoundland, Phillips took work as
a fish splitter. If any aspect of commercial fishing
can be said to be glamorous, fish-splitting is *not* it.
It is one of the smelliest and messiest jobs ever
invented by man. From morning 'til night, Phillips
sliced open the bellies of countless fish and tossed
them into a bin to be gutted and cleaned by someone else. It was the same mind-numbing action
over and over again. To a skilled carpenter, fish-
splitting was a demeaning step down in life—
brainless, undignified and above all, smelly.

To someone who'd once yearned to be a pirate, a
fish-splitting hut must have seemed like the very
bowels of hell itself. As he wielded the splitting
knife, every flick of his wrist made him think of
his unfulfilled ambitions. A thousand times a day
he was reminded of the better things that might
have been, and the staring eyes of the dead fish
bore indifferent witness to his failure. Whether
Phillips took up fish-splitting because he couldn't
find any work as a shipwright, or with a mind to
assemble a pirate crew, will never be known. But
soon he had found 16 other fish splitters who hated
their jobs as much as he did.

St. Peter's Harbour, Newfoundland (August 29, 1723)

John Phillips peered into the night and cursed under his breath. Where *were* they? He had painstakingly picked 16 men, all of whom had agreed to join him in the venture of stealing a ship and becoming pirates. They had made their plans carefully, setting their sights on a sturdy schooner moored in the harbour and owned by Mr. William Minot of Boston. And now the night agreed upon for the taking of the ship had arrived, but besides Phillips, a grand total of four aspiring pirates had actually shown up: John Nutt, James Sparks, Thomas Fern and William White—all desperate men who smelled of fish.

It says something about Phillips' utter hatred for fish-splitting that he decided to go ahead with his plan even though his band of conspirators numbered 12 less than he had been expecting. No matter—there was only one night watchman aboard the ship and five-to-one made good odds. Through some kind of ruse, the soon-to-be pirates lured the night watchman off the deck and left him on shore, bound and gagged. Then they cast off into the darkness.

As Phillips set sail into the blackness of night on the ocean, there were many things to think about: He would have to draft Articles of Agreement; the pirates would have to agree on who should fill which shipboard positions; they would have to rename the ship and, perhaps most importantly,

they definitely needed to find some more crewmen. Whether those crewmen *wanted* to be pirates
or not, John Phillips did not care.

They decided to rename the ship *Revenge*. Phillips became the captain; John Nutt was made navigator; Thomas Fern became the carpenter, and
William White served as the single ordinary crew
member. Next they drew up Articles of Agreement. These were fairly straightforward, setting
out how much treasure each man would get, rules
for shipboard life and so forth. But the ninth and
last article read: "If at any Time we meet with a
prudent Woman, that Man that offers to meddle
with her without her consent shall suffer present
Death." Clearly Phillips' experience with Anstis'
crew had left its mark on him. Since they couldn't
find a bible to swear the Articles of Agreement,
someone pulled out an axe and they swore on
that.

For the next few weeks, things went surprisingly well for these fledgling desperadoes. On
September 5, 1723, they captured a number of
fishing vessels off the shores of Newfoundland.
They also forced three crewmen to join forces with
them, including one named John Fillmore (whose
great-grandson Millard Fillmore would become
the 13th president of the United States). Their success continued when, later in September, they captured a schooner. After that they took a French
ship carrying a substantial cargo of wine as well as
a large cannon that the pirates transferred to their

own ship. They also impressed two additional crew members into service: Peter Taffrey and John Baptis.

Early in October they captured the *Mary* with a cargo worth £500, quickly followed by another ship from which they recruited their first willing volunteer, William Taylor. Taylor was an Englishman who had fallen into debt and was being shipped to Virginia to be sold into slavery. It's not hard to understand why becoming a pirate would have seemed preferable to slavery.

As their cruise took them farther south, they captured ship after ship, and Phillips' luck seemed to hold, in even the unlikeliest of situations. Running short of food and getting desperate, they went after a vessel that was much more heavily armed than any of their own. Sailing up alongside a 12-gun sloop out of Martinique, Phillips shouted that unless her crew surrendered immediately, they could expect no mercy from the pirates. To his surprise, the French sailors gave up right away. Phillips' raiders went aboard, took what supplies they wanted, forced four crewmen to join them and then let the vessel sail away.

At some point, a man named John Rose Archer joined Phillips' crew. Archer had sailed with a pirate who was a legend in his own lifetime: Edward Teach, also known as Blackbeard. Impressed with Archer's pirate resumé, Phillips immediately made him quartermaster of the *Revenge*. In practice, the

quartermaster was the second most powerful man
on the ship after the captain. The quartermaster
kept the records of all captured treasure and kept a
running tally of each man's share. The quartermaster also had considerable authority to settle
shipboard disputes and mete out punishment as
he saw fit. It was an important and prestigious
position on a pirate ship, or on any ship for that
matter. But in promoting Archer, Phillips angered
one of the four men who'd been with him from
the beginning: Thomas Fern, the carpenter.

Fern now joined forces with three other crewmen: James Woods, William Taylor (the man rescued from immanent slavery) and William Phillips
(no relation to his captain). Together they sailed
off in one of the vessels captured by the *Revenge*,
but Phillips quickly gave chase and sailed alongside, demanding that Fern surrender. Fern pulled
out his pistol and squeezed off a shot over the rails,
missing Phillips but making him very angry. A
brief skirmish followed in which James Woods
was killed, and the other Phillips (William) was
badly wounded in one leg.

Fern and Taylor surrendered, but there was still
the matter of William Phillips' injured leg. It was
clearly a lost cause and he was losing a lot of blood.
Even though he had tried to sail off in the stolen
ship, the crew of the *Revenge* took pity on the
wounded man; they decided to save his life by
amputating his leg. The pirates didn't have a surgeon

as such, but after all, the mutinous Fern *was* the ship's carpenter. Among the pirates, the general feeling was that this made him good at sawing things off. The rest of the crew sent Fern below decks and soon he reappeared with a saw that he judged right for cutting through bone. The wounded Phillips was given a cloth to bite down on, and Fern set to work hacking off his wounded leg. A few minutes and several blood-curdling screams later, the amputated limb lay beside its former owner on the deck of the ship.

To cauterize the wound, Fern heated a broad-axe until the blade was white hot and pressed the flat surface against the bloody end of the stump. With the searing smell of cooked meat, the wound was sealed shut. The most surprising thing about this gruesome operation is that it worked. Phillips' leg healed and he spent his recovery on board the *Revenge* for fear of being hanged if returned to land.

Despite his nascent skills as a doctor, when Fern tried to escape a second time, Captain Phillips took him ashore, tied him to a palm tree and shot him through the heart. Harsh though this punishment was, it was no more than was laid out in the Articles of Agreement. Article 2 stipulated that men who tried to escape would be marooned, and Article 3 directed that any pirate attempting to steal from the company at large would be shot.

The *Revenge* headed north and quickly captured two ships from Virginia, one of which was called the *Dolphin*. When Phillips went aboard the *Dolphin* to look her over, he was attacked by the vessel's captain, Robert Mortimer. Mortimer grabbed a metal handspike (used for loosening stubborn knots) and smashed it into Phillips' head. Amazingly, either because Mortimer had botched his swing or because Phillips had a hard head, the attack had little effect on Phillips, who drew his sword and ran Mortimer through with it. Two pirates from the *Revenge* promptly hacked Mortimer's body to pieces, which served to frighten the rest of the *Dolphin*'s crew into complete submission. Seemingly unfazed by this attack, Phillips set about deciding which of the captive crew he would impress into service on the *Revenge*. He chose two: seaman Charles Ivemay and carpenter Edward Cheeseman (the *Revenge* having been without a carpenter since Phillips killed Tern). Phillips sent John Fillmore to row Cheeseman back to the *Revenge*.

The dangerous thing about sailing around with a shipful of captive labour is that your prisoners have plenty of time to scheme about how to rebel. The men forced into service on the *Revenge* knew that if they were ever captured, everyone on board the ship would be made to stand trial, whether they were on the ship willingly or not. They also knew that judges would be more lenient towards men who had actually made some attempt at resistance.

By this time John Fillmore had been in Phillips' clutches for nearly eight months. Now, finding himself alone in a small boat with a new prisoner, he quickly explained that if they recruited one or two other men to their purpose, they could take control of the *Revenge*. In Cheeseman, Fillmore found a wholehearted ally. With this conspiracy now smouldering in her midst like a slowly burning fuse, the *Revenge* continued her east-coast rampage. She would go on to capture a further 11 vessels in the weeks that followed.

On April 14, 1724, Phillips captured a sloop called the *Squirrel*, under the command of her owner, Andrew Haraden. The *Squirrel* was brand new; she was so new that her decking was not completely finished. Nonetheless, she was a handsome prize, and Phillips decided to make her his new flagship. He transferred all of the supplies from the *Revenge* onto the *Squirrel* and switched crews as well. He set the *Squirrel*'s crew free in the *Revenge* and then went on his way in his new ship. But for some reason he elected to keep Captain Haraden with him on the *Squirrel*, and this was to lead to his downfall.

Haraden was highly motivated to get his ship back, and when Edward Cheeseman revealed his and Fillmore's plan to take control, Haraden immediately joined the band of mutineers. Some of the men wanted to stage their attack at night, but Cheeseman pointed out that a daylight attack had two key advantages: Not only would the pirates would be less likely to expect it, but there would also be less chance of confusion. Everyone saw the wisdom in this and they agreed that noon on April 17 would be zero hour.

April 17, 1724 – Noon

To John Nutt, pirate sailing master of the ship *Squirrel,* things were in an orderly way. The weather was calm and the sailing was smooth. The new men who had recently been forced to join the crew were fitting in as well. The new carpenter, Edward Cheeseman, was working to complete the unfinished deck, and even John Fillmore, the man held in captivity the longest, was helping him. The deck was littered with mallets, chisels, saws and axes all ready to hand if Cheeseman and Fillmore should need them. Even Haraden seemed to have accepted his fate and had made no complaint. Maybe they were growing used to the idea of spending the rest of their days as pirates. Cheeseman had even offered Nutt a friendly swig out of his brandy bottle and now the two of them were strolling around the deck with Fillmore picking up an axe to continue the work. But wait—what was that—had Haraden just winked at Cheeseman? Had some sort of signal passed between the two men?

But before Nutt could think further, Cheeseman grabbed him by the neck with one hand and reached down between the pirate's legs and grabbed Nutt's testicles with the other. Then the two of them scrambled across the deck, where Cheeseman threw the pirate overboard. At the last minute though, Nutt grabbed onto Cheeseman's sleeve and hung there, dangling over the edge of the ship.

"Lord have mercy upon me!" cried Nutt. "What are you trying to do, carpenter?"

"Master, you are a dead man," replied Cheeseman and struck Nutt a tremendous blow on the arm, and the pirate fell into the sea to drown.

For his part, Fillmore took the axe he had been holding and brought it crashing down on the head of another pirate, cleaving his head in half right down the neck. Warned by the commotion, Captain Phillips ran up from below decks, but by this time Cheeseman had picked up a mallet and smashed Phillips across the chin with it. Although this surely broke his jaw, the pirate kept on coming. Haraden now waded into the fray, but a pirate gunner, appropriately enough named Sparks, made to stop him. Cheeseman tripped the gunner whereupon he was thrown overboard by two of the other mutineers. This gave Haraden time to pick up an axe—possibly the very one that Phillips had sworn the Articles of Agreement on—and bury it in the pirate captain's skull, killing him instantly.

Meanwhile, Cheeseman had descended into the bowels of the ship to find Blackbeard's former lieutenant John Rose Archer. After finding Archer and smashing him over the head a couple of times with the mallet, Cheeseman was about to deliver the death blow when one of the other mutineers staid his hand—they had already killed 13 of the pirates. Surely it would be good have some of them alive to testify in evidence at the inevitable trial? Everyone saw the sense in this, and the surviving pirates were kept as prisoners until the *Squirrel* put into port.

Phillips captured 33 vessels in just under eight months. His final tally was three shallops, fifteen fishing vessels, three schooners, three brigantines, four sloops and five ships. Impressive as this was, Phillips was in no position to brag about it, what with being dead and all. The mutineers had cut off his head and hung it from the mast, later transferring it to a pickle barrel to be sent to Boston as evidence. At the trial, based on favourable testimony from Haraden, Edward Cheeseman and John Fillmore were acquitted of all charges. The other pirates were also either acquitted or pardoned with the exception of John Rose Archer and William White, who were both duly hanged in Boston.

And so ended the violent, if somewhat successful piratical career of John Phillips.

CHAPTER NINE

Ned and Margaret Jordan

Many a good hanging prevents a bad marriage.

–William Shakespeare, *Twelfth Night*

Off the Coast of Nova Scotia (September 13, 1809)

John Stairs, captain of the *Three Sisters,* was in a fight for his life. He had just gone below decks to consult a book when he looked up to see one of his passengers, Ned Jordan, aiming a pistol at him down through the skylight. He pulled back just as Jordan fired, but the bullet grazed his nose and cheek then smashed into seaman Thomas Heath who was standing nearby. Heath collapsed on the floor, crying, "Oh God, I am killed!"

Stairs wiped the stinging gunpowder off his face and turned to his sea chest where he kept a brace of pistols. He flipped it open only to discover that both guns were gone. Had Ned Jordan taken them? There was no time for wondering—he needed some sort of weapon, if not a gun then at least a blade. Captain Stairs rooted around in the trunk for his cutlass, but it was gone too. Then he heard four or five pistol shots ring out from above.

Armed or not, Stairs knew he had to get up on deck to find out what the devil was going on. He started up the ladder but met Ned Jordan coming down. Captain Stairs describes the encounter in his own words:

> On going up the ladder I met...Edward Jordan, in the act of descending; one of his feet was on the ladder; he held an axe in his right hand, and a pistol in his left. I seized his arms, and, begging him for God's sake to spare my life, shoved him backwards, when he snapped the pistol; I instantly grasped it by the muzzle, wrested it from him, and threw it overboard; and called Kelly the mate to my assistance, but he made me no answer. Benjamin Matthews came hastily aft, he appeared to be wounded, and fell down. By this time I had taken the axe from Jordan, and endeavoured to strike him, but he held me so forcibly as to prevent me. I, however, threw the axe overboard.

At this point Captain Stairs had managed to disarm Ned Jordan, but he hadn't counted on Ned's wife, Margaret, who suddenly appeared, shrieking like a banshee and brandishing a boathook. "It is Kelly you want," she screamed, "I'll give you Kelly." Then she set about hitting Stairs with the handle of the boathook. Between blows from Margaret Jordan, Stairs had managed to notice three very disturbing things: First, seaman Benjamin Matthews lay where he had fallen, showing no signs of life—this would explain the pistol shots he had heard earlier. Second, the wounded seaman Heath had somehow managed to come up from below, but now he too lay lifeless on the starboard side of the deck. Third, his first mate, John Kelly, was not even trying to help him. What was going on here?

Disentangling himself from the Jordans at last, Stairs watched as Ned Jordan stalked to the stern of the ship and picked up another axe. Then Jordan walked over to where Matthews lay unconscious and struck him several gory blows in the back of the head with the business end of the axe. Through this entire ordeal, Captain Stairs seems to have remained remarkably clear-headed. Realizing that the Jordans were going to kill him, he spied a wooden hatch cover sitting loose on the deck nearby. The hatch would certainly float, and though it was no lifeboat, it would have to do. In the next couple of seconds he made his decision: "Finding no chance of my life if I remained on board, and that I might as well be drowned as shot, I threw the hatch overboard, jumped after it."

The story of Ned Jordan's life is not a happy one. He had been born sometime around 1771 in County Carlo, Ireland. In 1797 he was sentenced to death for "exercising men in the night" (that is, secretly training militia) with a view to taking part in a rebellion. He joined the army to escape the death sentence, married Margaret and decided to make a fresh start in the New World. Once landed in North America, they lived first in New

York, then Montréal and finally settled in the coastal village of Percé, Québec. Here Ned had a bit of success as a fisherman and, probably for the first time in his life, was bringing home a decent wage. In the meantime, he and Margaret had started a family, producing three little girls and later, a son. Wanting to make a better life for his children, Ned set about building his own boat and named it for his daughters: *Three Sisters*. But soon he ran into money problems and was forced to mortgage his ship to a pair of Halifax moneylenders, the Tremain brothers.

In the end, Ned couldn't repay the money, and the Tremains were about to take possession of the ship when Ned convinced them to let him make one last run from Halifax back to Percé. There, he said, he was collecting a huge shipment of fish that would more than pay his debt to them. They agreed, but insisted on sending their own captain with Jordan to oversee the voyage—the man they chose was Captain Stairs. The Tremains' suspicions were well founded, since Jordan's plan the whole time was to steal the *Three Sisters* and sail back to Ireland. Arriving in Percé, Jordan had picked up Margaret and the children, probably telling Captain Stairs that they were all going to spend some time in Halifax. Now the whole unhappy family was on board.

And what of Margaret Jordan? Some have portrayed her as a sort of femme fatale, using her considerable wiles to seduce half the crew of the *Three*

Sisters, enabling her husband to stage his coup. Others have suggested that Ned himself put her up to flirting with first mate John Kelly in order to secure his co-operation. In other versions of the tale, Margaret's ravishing beauty causes trouble on board as everyone (including Stairs) begins jealously bickering over her. However, the story that comes through in the court transcripts is far more mundane. Here we meet a woman suffering indifference and abuse at the hands of a husband driven to drink and despair when his business plans fall apart and debt begins to mount. Furthermore, as his plans went from bad to worse, Ned seems to have become completely unhinged. He became suspicious of Margaret, viewing her as a liability, since she was privy to all of his plans and crimes.

In the meantime, Margaret had four small children to care for, and many of the troubles on board the *Three Sisters* seem to stem from the rest of the men merely being sympathetic to her situation. From Captain Stairs she asked for and received a bolt of fabric to make some new clothes for her little girls. This threw Ned into a jealous rage and prompted his attempted shooting of Stairs, resulting in the accidental death of Heath.

To other crew members Margaret confessed that she was worried Ned wanted to kill her, and she sought their protection. She later confessed that when she attacked Captain Stairs with the boathook, she was out of her mind with stress, fear and anxiety. One gets the sense that she went along with her husband's wild plans because she simply felt she had no other choice. And although her relationship with John Kelly, the first mate, remains ambiguous, one thing is for certain: John Kelly himself was indeed part of the plot to take control of the *Three Sisters*.

Ned Jordan and John Kelly leaned over the rail of the *Three Sisters* and watched as Stairs wrapped his arms around the hatch cover and clung for dear life. Jordan cocked a pistol and aimed it down at the defenceless man floating in the sea below. Kelly, however, stopped him, explaining that Stairs would either freeze to death or drown before very long, and Jordan ought not to waste his shot. And so Jordan lowered his gun, confident that he had seen the last of Captain Stairs.

The first part of Jordan's plot had gone more or less according to plan; the *Three Sisters* had completed the first leg of her voyage from Halifax to Percé. But once in Percé, Captain Stairs had immediately seen that the shipment of fish they were supposed to pick up was not as large as Jordan had claimed. It had clearly been a ruse to get Jordan back to Percé to collect his wife and children. Although he must have been suspicious, Stairs allowed Jordan to bring his family aboard for the return trip to Halifax. Possibly, he felt sorry for them. Possibly he was attracted to Margaret as later accounts suggest. Either way, Stairs was a danger to

Jordan since he would report back to the Tremains that Jordan had no way of making good his debt.

However, with Stairs now floating in their wake and doomed to die a slow, cold death, all those problems had vanished. Jordan and Kelly threw the dead bodies of Heath and Matthews overboard. They had gotten rid of the evidence and eliminated a chief witness against them, but now another difficulty arose—with Stairs gone, they had no one on board who knew how to navigate. This presented a distinct problem, because now Jordan wanted to sail back to Ireland—a tricky feat without a navigator. There was only one thing to do: They would have to put into port somewhere and trick a navigator into coming with them.

They put in at Little Bay, an inlet of Fortune Bay on Newfoundland's south coast. John Kelly now called himself Captain John Stairs, and Ned Jordan presented himself as one of the Tremains, the rightful owners of the *Three Sisters*. They failed to find a navigator but succeeded in bullying one John Pigot into joining the crew. Pigot had been on board the *Three Sisters* for a look around. Clearly this was a ship in no way engaged in the business of fishing; the fish weren't even packed properly, just strewn about haphazardly. Pigot correctly assumed that there was something fishy going on and refused to sign on. Kelly and Jordan then found a justice of the peace and somehow convinced him to threaten Pigot with being clapped in irons and tied to a flagstaff unless he joined the crew. Faced with imprisonment and public humiliation, the suspicious Pigot reluctantly signed on.

The *Three Sisters* then sailed south and east, across the wide mouth of Placentia Bay until she arrived at St. Mary's. Here she stayed for six or seven days while Jordan looked in vain for a navigator. When he didn't find one, Pigot and the others refused to go any further. It was during this time that Pigot first discovered that the man he knew as Tremain was actually named Jordan. Finally Jordan managed to find a pilot who did at least know the way to St. John's, and the unhappy group set off to look for a navigator there.

Luck was not with them though, for no sooner had they left the harbour at St. Mary's than the wind failed and they were becalmed. Jordan hitched a ride on a passing vessel that was also heading for St. John's. Leaving his ship and his family, Jordan went with Pigot on the new ship to continue his quest for a navigator. Arriving in St. John's they finally found a navigator who could get them to Ireland: Patrick Power. Power signed on for the wage of £11 per month for as long as the voyage lasted.

Now in St. John's, they needed some way to get back to the *Three Sisters*. This meant hiring a small vessel and some boatmen to take them south along the coast to the Bay of Bulls, where Jordan reckoned he had left the ship. Jordan, however, was reluctant to go out in the streets of St. John's to help Power look for men with a boat. He explained that he owed money there and could not run the risk of being spotted.

After three days of making inquiries by himself, Power at last found two men with a small boat who were willing to make the voyage. With the promise of £10 for their troubles, the boatmen loaded Jordan, Power and Pigot into their vessel and set off to look for the *Three Sisters*. But when the trio arrived at the Bay of Bulls, the *Three Sisters* was not there. They persuaded the boatmen to take them next to Agua Fort, where Jordan said he was sure they would find the ship. Next, they sailed to Agua Fort, but there was still no sign of the *Three Sisters*. Finally they cajoled the boatmen into taking them as far as Trepassey, where at last Jordan found his ship.

Thus began the strangest three days and nights in Patrick Power's life. The men finally boarded the *Three Sisters* about half an hour after dark, and trouble began right away. Margaret Jordan didn't seem to be anywhere on board, and John Kelly said she had gone ashore in Trepassey. According to Power, upon hearing this, Jordan was "much disturbed." Jordan and Kelly rowed ashore and presently returned with Margaret. Jordan himself went to bed almost immediately.

Pigot, Kelly and Power sat up in the cabin drinking grog and talking. Margaret sat nearby. Before long Jordan sprang up from his bunk and said to

Margaret, "You whore! I heard you talk!" Then he pulled down a musket from the wall, whereupon Margaret screeched at Power to take it away from him. Wrestling the gun away from his employer, Power took it above decks and went over to the boatmen who'd brought them from St. John. Their little boat was still moored alongside the *Three Sisters* because they were waiting for Jordan to pay them. Power gave them the musket and told them to keep a close eye on it.

Power got back to the cabin just in time to find Jordan and Kelly punching each other and arguing. Jordan accused Kelly and his wife of spending too much time ashore together. Furthermore, Jordan demanded that Kelly relinquish Jordan's pistols so that he could shoot his wife. And then to Power's amazement, Kelly actually produced the pistols and held them out, one in each hand. Power grabbed them away from him and followed Margaret up on deck. He told her that he was going to entrust the pistols to the boatmen for safekeeping. Margaret, however, asked him several times to throw the weapons overboard, saying, "You know not the mischief they have done!"

Then Kelly came on deck and explained to Power that the only reason *he* had the guns was so that Jordan *wouldn't* have them. He also told Power where there was a second musket, which was promptly confiscated and also given to the boatmen. We can only wonder what the boatmen themselves thought of all this. First they take three strange men on a wild goose chase up the coast looking for a ship that doesn't seem to exist. Then they find the ship, but have to wait all night for payment. And during the night, one of their would-be employers keeps coming out and giving them guns to look after.

Meanwhile, Margaret told Power that if he gave her husband some rum it would put him to sleep. Returning to the cabin, Power found Jordan in a belligerent mood and promptly dosed him with rum, upon which he began to fall asleep. As he dozed off, he said to Power, "Do not let my wife come to bed with me. If you do, I shall kill her." And so ended Patrick Power's first night aboard the *Three Sisters.*

The next day, Power was up early and chanced to overhear Margaret Jordan repeatedly begging Pigot to take her ashore because she was convinced her husband would kill her if she stayed on board any longer. Then she approached Power and repeated her entreaties, but he too refused. She turned to him and said, "You know not the life I lead with that man...he will kill me before we get to Ireland. You had better let me go ashore; you are a stranger to my suffering. Pigot can describe to you the cruel life I lead with that man."

About an hour after sunrise, Jordan appeared on deck and charged at Margaret. Power threw himself between them, whereupon Ned grasped his lapels and demanded the return of his pistols.

Margaret began slapping Power on the back and shrieking for him not to let her husband kill her and that if she died it was Power's fault for not letting her go ashore.

Now Jordan accused his wife of sharing her bed with not only the Power, but the entire rest of the crew. "I believe, Power, you have been with her all night, as well as the rest," sneered Ned Jordan. Patrick Power by this point had had enough and told Jordan to do with his wife as he pleased. There followed a repeat of the first act, with Jordan rushing at Margaret, Margaret begging Power to protect her, and Power doing his best to keep his employer from hitting his wife. Finally, Power got them calmed down, and Jordan promised that if Margaret would go into the cabin with him they would talk calmly and he would not hurt her. Surprisingly, the warring couple came to some sort of agreement and were on good terms for the rest of the day.

But no sooner had Power gotten the battling Jordans sorted out than the boatmen appeared on deck demanding the £10 that Jordan had promised them. Power dutifully went off and found Jordan, who told his new navigator that he didn't have the money to pay the boatmen. If Power would look in the forward hold he would find some leather that he could give them instead. Not surprisingly, the boatmen were having none of it, and so Jordan offered them not only the leather but also his watch. Since the doubtless bewildered boatmen do not appear again in the court transcripts, we have to assume that they took the leather and the watch and left (maybe they got to keep the guns too).

Surprisingly, even after all this chaos, Patrick Power set about trying to make the ship ready for an actual voyage to Ireland. He had made the crossing many times and knew both the kind and quantity of supplies needed for such a journey, none of which he found on the *Three Sisters*, aside from a quantity of badly stowed fish. At this point, in his own words, he "began to suspect some mischief." Nonetheless, this floating circus of dysfunction and suspicion got under way and returned to the Bay of Bulls, where Jordan claimed to have a friend who would outfit them with supplies. When they finally dropped anchor between 10 and 11 that night, Power must have been wondering whether *any* amount of money was worth all this trouble, never mind £11 a month.

The next day was the same as the first—but a whole lot louder and a whole lot worse. There were series of trips ashore by Jordan and various members of the crew to bring back supplies. At one point, Power allowed Margaret to go ashore to do some laundry, and Ned was very upset when he found out. As the day progressed, Ned's plan began to further unravel. There was no wind and so he went ashore and returned with several men to row his ship out to sea where the breezes were stronger. He was also in a great panic, saying that a ship was on its way from Halifax to take him prisoner because of the money he owed.

Power now flatly refused to leave the harbour, and all of the rowers went back to the mainland. Ned became openly hostile towards Power, saying he regretted hiring him in the first place. Power said he would be just as happy to quit. Tension between the two only worsened when Jordan overheard a discussion between Power and Kelly: Kelly said that if Power would agree to go ashore with him, Kelly would tell him an important piece of information. Power agreed, but now Jordan was suspicious of the two men and refused to go to bed until both of them had gone to bed as well.

The next morning marked the third day that Patrick Power had been employed at this strange job—it was also to be his last. As day broke, Ned Jordan ordered Power to haul up the anchor and get under way. Power went up on deck and now, possibly stalling, said that the wind was too strong to safely leave the harbour. Hearing this, Jordan had a veritable conniption and stormed off. Then, sitting in his cabin, Power heard someone say that Kelly had made off with the little cutter used for ferrying back and forth between the ship and the shore. Power rushed up on deck to see that Kelly had indeed taken the boat and was about 20 yards from the ship and making for shore. Power called to him to come back, and Kelly answered that he would return for Power shortly. Power had had enough and went back to his cabin to gather up his things and await Kelly's return. But now he heard someone up on deck say the anchor cable had been cut! He rushed above decks again and saw Jordan standing with an axe—he had cut the *Three Sisters'* anchor cable, and now she was adrift.

Having no choice, Power now raised canvas and grudgingly set sail. Before long though, a sail appeared on the horizon and Jordan became greatly agitated. The ship drew alongside and proved to be the *HMS Cuttle* commanded by Lieutenant Bury. Bury announced that Ned Jordan was hereby under arrest for piracy and murder. On what evidence, Jordan wanted to know. Came the reply: Why, based on the testimony of Captain John Stairs of course! We can only imagine what ran through Jordan's mind when he heard this. A man he had assumed drowned or frozen to death had seemingly just come back from the dead to put a noose around his neck.

And this is perhaps the most amazing part of this strange tale. Upon jumping overboard, Captain Stairs had clung to the hatch in the icy waters for about three hours and had pretty much assumed he was done for. But then a sail appeared, and before he knew it, he had been rescued by an American schooner bound for Massachusetts. Captain Stairs made his way to Boston and there told the story of what Jordan had done. By the time of his capture, ships up and down the eastern seaboard had been warned to keep an eye out for the *Three Sisters*.

The trial was Canada's first for piracy. Testimony revealed that throughout the entire ordeal, all four of the Jordan children had been on board the *Three Sisters*, seemingly unaware of what was happening. It was probably for their sake, as much as her own, that Margaret Jordan was acquitted of the charges against her, since the judge had no wish to orphan four children. Their father, however, was sentenced to death, and Ned Jordan was hanged on November 24, 1809. The clergyman in attendance said Jordan seemed genuinely repentant for what he had done.

Ned Jordan's story is a sad one, all the more so since it seems to stem from a genuine desire to make a better life for his family. But like many frustrated providers before and since, Jordan over-extended himself, and his plans failed. Then he watched his hopes drain away in a downward spiral of misfortune, debt and drink. As circumstances spun out of control, he came to feel that he had no choice but to commit murder in order to further his plans—and when he fired the shot that killed John Heath, the trapdoor of the gallows had already opened beneath him.

CHAPTER TEN

Fielding & Son

Murder will out, this is my conclusion.

–Geoffery Chaucer

ON MAY 28, 1844, THE FOLLOWING HEADLINE BLARED FROM
the front page of the *Halifax Morning Post*:

Extraordinary Shipwreck

Wreck of the Barque Saladin, on the Coast of Nova Scotia, with a cargo of PURE SILVER! ROUND DOLLARS!!

Copper and Guano

FULL PARTICULARS!!!

Halifax of 1844 was a busy seaport, with a reputation as an up-and-coming centre on the east
coast. It was large enough to support at least four
newspapers: the *Nova Scotian,* the *Morning Chronicle,*
the *Times* and of course, the *Halifax Morning Post*.
Haligonians of the day could read a wide selection
of news from at home and abroad. They would
have enjoyed their fair share of lurid stories about
theft, murder and mysterious goings-on. But even
these seasoned readers were scrambling over themselves to get the next installment of the *Saladin*
story—it was 1844's equivalent of must-see TV.

As the details of the *Saladin* slowly emerged, the answers only seemed to raise more questions: Why had the crew of a perfectly seaworthy vessel allowed her to wash up on shore? And why were there only six crewmen found on board when the *Saladin* had set sail with 14? Was it true that most of the six had been drunk when the ship was discovered. Was it also true that a suit of boy's clothes had been found on board? Where was the boy who should have been wearing them? What about the rumours of a substantial fortune in silver bars and coins said to be in the ship's hold? And swirling through the conjectures, the suppositions and even the facts, was one enjoyably dangerous word—pirates!

On May 25, 1844, the beached hulk of the *Saladin* was discovered by local townsfolk near Country Harbour, Nova Scotia. She was found on Harbour Island to the rear of the bay, on a tip of land that has since become known as Saladin Point. The locals promptly informed Captain Cunningham of the schooner *Billow*, who was nearby on business. As Cunningham got closer, he could see men on the deck of the beached ship. One of them shouted for the captain to please come aboard and take command. They had all drunk too much grog, bellowed the man, and needed someone to assist them. The winds were high and the waters rough, so one of the men threw a rope from the mysterious vessel to the deck of the *Billow.* Captain Cunningham tied the line around his waist, jumped into the sea and the stranded men pulled him through the crashing waves to shore, whereupon he clambered up on to the deck of their ship.

Once on board, Cunningham discovered a bizarre state of affairs. The ship was the *Saladin*, bound from Valparaiso (Chile's main seaport) to London, England. On board were 70 tons of copper, 13 bars of silver weighing 150 pounds apiece and a large quantity of spice valued at $9000. But the majority of the *Saladin*'s cargo was guano. "Guano" is the polite term for bat and bird droppings. Because it contains a lot of phosphorous and nitrogen, guano used to be a key ingredient in the manufacture of gunpowder. It also makes an excellent fertilizer when spread on the surface of barren soil. And this was why the *Saladin* was laden with what amounted to several tons of feces—valuable feces, but feces nonetheless.

Besides being obviously the worse for drink, the six men on board the *Saladin* told an unlikely tale: The captain had died some seven or eight weeks earlier, the first officer had died three days after that, and the second officer had become deceased around the same time. The rest of the crew had either fallen into the sea and drowned or had been killed. No further explanation was given. Upon entering the cabin, Cunningham found a wild scattering of men's clothing, navigational instruments that had been taken apart (seemingly out of curiosity), and finally, an open sea chest sitting in the middle of the room and overflowing with silver dollars!

Unable to get any sense out of the men on board, Cunningham cut off their supply of grog and set about salvaging everything he could. He made an inventory of everything in the hold and had all the sail and rigging removed, then turned the whole thing over to a local justice of the peace and went on his way. The schooner *Fair Rosemont* was dispatched to transport the goods and crew back to Halifax. There, the six men found on board were clapped into irons and thrown into jail, their stories yet to be told.

The key player in this mysterious tale was a desperate ruffian named George Fielding. As well as being a sea captain, Fielding was also a sort of professional desperado. Indeed, after the events on board the *Saladin,* an acquaintance expressed surprise that he was not hanged 20 years earlier. Fielding had been born in the British Isles but was brought up in Gaspé. As a young man he got his sea legs on vessels in and out of Newfoundland seaports. He seems to have been an able enough sailor and eventually earned his own command. As commander of the merchant ship *Vitula,* Fielding hauled a large cargo of guano from the Peruvian island of Chincha back to Liverpool, Nova Scotia, for local merchants Myers & Co.

In October 1842 he set sail in the *Vitula* for Buenos Ayres, expecting to pick up another cargo of guano. But once there, he discovered that the guano yield had been low and there was nothing for him to haul. At this point he could have easily returned to Canadian waters, but instead he sailed on to Valparaiso in the hopes of finding cargo there. When the docks of Valparaiso proved as unprofitable as those at Buenos Ayres, Fielding made plans to smuggle a cargo of guano out of Peru. Unfortunately the authorities immediately got wind of the scheme and sent a schooner with 50 soldiers on board to arrest him.

Arriving at the harbour where the *Vitula* was anchored, the Peruvian troops quickly came up with a plan. One of them swam out to the ship, cut loose the longboat she towed behind her and took it back to their schooner. Then the soldiers used this little craft to ferry a boatload of men over to the moored ship. Fielding quickly realized what was happening and brought an armload of muskets up onto the deck in the hopes that his crew would fight back. But on seeing the soldiers, his crew lost their nerve and fled below decks.

Now it was just Fielding and his son, who was about 13 years old and also named George. Fielding realized that the only thing to do was to try to get away—and quickly. But here they had another problem; the anchor was too large and heavy for a man and a boy to haul up by themselves. With his crew cowering below decks, and the soldiers drawing steadily closer, Fielding pulled out a knife and started sawing at the rope that connected to the ship to the anchor. If he could just cut through it fast enough then the *Vitula* might at least drift away from the clutches of this brigade of boat-stealing Peruvians. But before he could finish the job, he heard a sound across the deck and looked up to see the first soldier clambering over the rail. It was too late—he had been boarded! There was a short scuffle, during which Fielding was shot in the shoulder; he surrendered.

The description we have of George Fielding tells of a well-built man with a strong, decisive face, by no means unpleasant in his demeanour. From his years at sea he could speak a smattering of French, Spanish, Portuguese and Dutch. All in all he was a forceful, persuasive personality who probably had a convincing manner with people.

The Peruvian schooner took the *Vitula* back to Lima where the entire crew was thrown into jail on shore, except for Fielding. For some reason the authorities opted to keep him in custody on board his ship, anchored in the harbour. And now, held prisoner on a ship he once commanded, Fielding attempted to put his natural force of personality to work. He asked the very men guarding him if some of them would be willing to conspire with him to cut the *Vitula*'s anchor cable in the middle of the night, enabling them all to get away. The guards reported his overtures to the authorities and he was thrown in a proper jail on the mainland.

But George Fielding Sr. was by no means beaten yet. From inside the jail, he managed to make contact with George Jr. and had the boy smuggle in a poncho like the ones worn by the locals. Disguised by the poncho, he managed to escape from jail and spent two days hiding in a huge pile of wood shavings while the authorities scoured the town for him. Next, he and his son appear to have stowed away on a British vessel at anchor in the harbour and made their way to Valparaiso. There, Fielding approached two captains and asked for a free ride back to Canada. Both refused, but on his third try, he got lucky.

Fielding approached Alexander McKenzie of the *Saladin* and asked for passage. Captain McKenzie was, by all accounts, a harsh and unkind character who drank heavily. One of his crew called him the "most severe and dissatisfied master" he had ever sailed under. It is possible that McKenzie hoped to extract a bit of free labour from this experienced sailor and his son, but whatever his reasons, McKenzie granted them passage on the *Saladin,* and they set sail from Valparaiso on February 8, 1844.

As well as Captain McKenzie and the Fieldings, there were 11 other crew members on board when the *Saladin* left Peru. By the time she was discovered four months later in Nova Scotia, there were only six men on board. All of them were promptly thrown in jail and put on trial for piracy and murder. In the days before television, newspaper reports gave careful attention to the appearances of the players. The eyewitness accounts of the day provide an unusually complete description of the six surviving men who went to trial.

George Jones was a sail maker and later, the *Saladin*'s steward. He was an unsavoury sort, who actually had a wooden leg, and was described thusly: "...lowering eye-brows, and full blue eyes, with a countenance expressive of suspicion and treachery."

William Johnston, able seaman, age 23, confessed that his real name was William Trevaskiss. Said the *Acadian Recorder*, "His eyes are dark blue and his complexion sandy, with a bold, determined, and rather forbidding expression of countenance. He can read and write a little."

Charles Augustus Anderson, age 19, was a Swede, described as "well made," with dark hair and keen brown eyes: "His complexion is swarthy and his countenance prepossessing, yet there is enough of fire in his eye to indicate strong and easily excited passions.... he can read and write well in his own language."

William Carr, the *Saladin*'s cook, was a middle-aged man with light blue eyes and a fair complexion: "His countenance expresses determination and intelligence.... He can read and write, and carries with him a pocket bible, well-worn...He is a widower with two children looking up to him for support."

John Galloway, age 19, "has a prominent forehead, and a keen grey eye.... He can read and write well."

But the *Recorder* gave the most ink to crewman John Hazleton, age 28: "His complexion is dark, with smooth skin, and black hair and wiskers... reaching down to his chin and neatly trimmed. His eyes are large, full and dark and the expression of his countenance decidedly bad...he wears a large red woollen cap, a black neckerchief is thrown loosely over a white shirt, which being open at the breast displays a fine lambs wool guernsey, his throat from the chest up being bare. He is the beau-ideal of a pirate: bold, daring and reckless."

And with the stage set, the story of the voyage began.

At the beginning of April 1844, after they had been at sea for about two months, Fielding was up to his old tricks. The *Saladin* was carrying a valuable cargo, and if Fielding could gain control of the ship, he could profit greatly. He first approached George Jones, the man with the wooden leg, and explained his plan: Duty on the *Saladin* was divided into two watches, in effect, a day shift and a night shift. Therefore, at any given time, half of the crew was asleep below decks, resting from the day's work. Fielding wanted Jones to help him recruit mutineers from both watches—this way they could kill most of one watch, while the other watch was asleep. Then, when the second watch came on duty, they too would be killed.

It was a ruthless plan, and it worked surprisingly well. With Jones' help, Fielding recruited Hazleton, Trevaskiss (alias, Johnston) and the Swede, Anderson. At around midnight between April 13 and 14, Fielding rounded up his little ring of conspirators and told them, "This night it must be done." The second watch was scheduled to come on duty at 4 AM. This would give them about four hours to put the first phase of the plan into effect.

The first to die was the mate, Thomas Byerby. He had complained of feeling unwell and gone to lie down on a chicken coop. Trevaskiss, Anderson, Hazelton and Fielding silently grabbed a couple of broadaxes and surrounded the sleeping man. Then two of them (probably Anderson and Trevaskiss) smashed in his skull with the axes and rained down blows on the rest of his body. The four men then threw the battered body overboard and moved on to their next victim.

From the deck, Fielding could see down through a skylight into a cabin where Captain McKenzie lay sleeping. He sent Trevaskiss, Anderson and Hazleton down below to kill the captain, and they silently descended the ladder to do Fielding's bidding. Upon entering the cabin, the men came face to face with McKenzie's brown dog, sleeping next to its master. At the trial, all of the prisoners gave conflicting testimony, each trying to lay the guilt on others. But the one consistent piece of testimony was that they were afraid of being attacked by the dog, who immediately sat up and growled at the intruders. The three murderous pirates stopped cold and silently backtracked up the ladder to return to the deck. McKenzie continued to sleep peacefully.

It says something about these desperadoes that they had already killed one man, wanted to kill a second and yet it does not seem to have occurred to them to kill the dog. Maybe they realized that one good bark from the dog might wake the rest of the crew. But it's more likely that they were simply too drunk to think straight, since Fielding had plied them well with rum and brandy before the night's work began.

Fielding realized that they would have to kill Captain McKenzie later and decided to move on. He had Trevaskiss call down and wake the carpenter, asking him to come up on deck. Not suspecting anything amiss, the carpenter roused himself and started up the ladder. But as he set foot on deck, Anderson smashed an axe into the back of his head. Amazingly, the carpenter was only stunned, and, seeing this, Trevaskiss clapped one hand over their victim's mouth and the other to the back of his wounded head. Anderson and Hazleton helped throw the unconscious man overboard. The cold Atlantic water woke-up the carpenter though, and as he drifted in the *Saladin's* wake he loudly called, "Murder!" several times, before succumbing to the waves.

Seeing his chance, Fielding shouted, "Man overboard!" (or had Jones do it) to wake the ship's master. Upon hearing the shouts, Captain McKenzie ran up on deck in his nightshirt and was immediately attacked by the axe-wielding Anderson.

The first blow hit him in the shoulder and only served to make the captain angry: "You ruffian!" he exclaimed to Anderson, "I will take your life."

At this point the peg-legged Jones left his post at the wheel, clomped over to McKenzie and grabbed him by the head, while Anderson pinioned his arms. Fielding then grabbed an axe and hit McKenzie with it. McKenzie looked up at Fielding and gasped, "Oh Captain Fielding, do not do it."

"Oh damn you, I will give it to you!" snarled Fielding and proceeded to hit the captain with the axe until he was dead.

All the while, George Jr. stood by urging his father to "Give it to him!" Once all signs of life had left McKenzie's battered body, the four pirates heaved the corpse overboard into the darkness.

Panting from his exertions, Fielding turned to the men and rasped, "The ship is ours!" Then, wanting to secure Captain McKenzie's cabin for himself, he sent his son below with a carving knife and ordered him to stab any man who tried to enter. The fate of the dog is unknown.

With the captain out of the way, Fielding now called the new watch on deck. First up was seaman James Allen. It is interesting to note that if they couldn't attack sleeping men, the pirates tried to make sure that their victims' hands were busy. As James Allen arrived, Hazleton tried to give him a rope to tie off so that his hands would not be free. Allen replied that he first had to "obey a call of nature" and proceeded to the stern where he leaned over and started to pee. Anderson, realizing that Allen's hands were now busy with a task more absorbing than tying off any rope, picked up a claw hammer and approached the unsuspecting sailor from behind. Anderson dealt the back of Allen's head a terrific blow, and his body was heaved overboard. Jones once again took the wheel.

Next to arrive to stand their watch were seamen Thomas Moffat and Sam Collins. Collins immediately went to the head to relieve himself, and Anderson followed him, armed with a hammer. Meanwhile, Moffat sat down for a minute before starting work, whereupon Hazleton and Johnson attacked him with axes, spilling a great deal of his blood, which covered most of the starboard deck. They quickly pitched Moffat's body overboard and yelled forward to Anderson to kill Collins. Just as he had with Allen, Anderson waited until Collins was peeing, snuck up behind him, smashed his skull with the hammer and then threw the body overboard.

When ship's cook William Carr woke up the next day, he sensed something was wrong before he had even set foot on deck.

"What is the matter?" he asked from the hatchway.

"Come up," said one of the pirates. "We will not hurt you."

Emerging on to the deck, Carr at once saw the bloodstained deck and noticed the bloody axes and carpenter's tools strewn about.

"What is the matter?" he asked again.

"I am the commander of this vessel now," said Captain Fielding. "The master and crew have gone away and left us." Upon hearing this, Carr looked around and, being no fool, immediately saw that both the *Saladin*'s jolly boat and longboat were still in place.

"It is impossible," said Carr. "It can't be the case, for all the boats are still about the ship." Seeing that Carr could not be fooled, Fielding told him what had happened. When seaman John Galloway came on deck a little later, the pirates repeated their story to him.

With Carr and Galloway fearfully doing as they were told, the pirates now sat down to breakfast, all the while bragging about who was the best murderer. Seemingly it was Anderson, who helped to kill five out of the six men they had murdered. Next they went to the captain's cabin and began tearing open letters from the mail packet that the *Saladin* had been delivering. Many of the letters contained money, and they extracted whatever coins and bills they could find.

A short while later, Fielding sidled up to Galloway and suggested that they should kill all the others (except George Jr., of course) and then split the fortune between them. Fielding may have chosen Galloway because he had learned that, of the survivors, Galloway was the only one who knew how to navigate. Whatever his reasons, Fielding was in for a disappointment when Galloway refused. Next, Fielding approached one of his fellow mutineers, the murderous Swede, Charles Anderson. Upon hearing Fielding's treacherous plot, Anderson went straight to the other conspirators and told them. They immediately tied up Fielding and searched his cabin. They found a pair of hidden pistols, a butcher's knife that had gone missing as well as two bottles of brandy that they strongly suspected of being poisoned. In light of this, one can't help but wonder if Fielding had somehow poisoned first mate Thomas Byerby, who complained of feeling unwell before lying down for his final rest on the chicken coop.

It was quickly decided that Fielding and his son would be thrown overboard. But for some reason, bloodied as their hands were, none of the pirates wanted to do it; they wanted Carr and Galloway to do it instead. It seems unlikely that they had lost their nerve for killing; more probably they wanted to ensure Carr and Galloway's silence by making murderers of them too. Standing there before the Fieldings, Galloway wanted nothing to do with it, but Carr spoke to him saying, "John, we are in the hands of our enemies, we must either die or live, and must do something to save our lives." Seeming to see the reason in this, Galloway relented, and together they threw first Captain Fielding overboard and then his son.

With just the six of them left, the pirates transferred all of the money on board in to one chest. Their plan was to sink the *Saladin* and escape with the money in one of her small boats. But before they could affect this plan, their ship ran aground in Nova Scotia, and it is here that our tale began.

By the 1840s, the "Golden Age of Piracy" had been over for 120 years, and so a trial involving real, live pirates, one of whom had an actual wooden leg and another of whom was "bold, daring and reckless," captured the public's imagination. It was a field day for the lawyers too, with the prosecuting attorney general making the following grand pronouncement:

> *You will bear in mind that this is not a case affecting only our lives or property, but one in which the whole world is interested. Now that Commerce is extending her relations into every portion of the globe, and every sea is whitening with her sails, it is our duty to throw the protection of the law around those who go down to the*

*sea in ships—it is that alone which can give secu-
rity to the mariner and guard the interests of the
whole civilized world.*

Once the lawyers had finished explaining how
they were saving "the whole civilized world," the
trial itself got underway. The perpetrators admitted they had been quite drunk when the killing
was done and that their memories might be addled
by booze. But it quickly became apparent that
Jones and Hazleton in particular were doing
everything in their power to suggest that Fielding
had frightened or threatened them into doing his
bidding. Oddly enough, Anderson, the pirate with
the most blood on his hands, made a relatively full
and honest confession. Combined with the testimony of Carr and Galloway, it provided a relatively
clear picture of what had happened during that
bloody night on the *Saladin*.

Jones, Trevaskiss, Anderson and Hazleton were
found guilty and were hanged on July 30, 1844.
A huge crowd turned out for the hanging, which
took place on a hill to the rear of Halifax's Catholic
cemetery. Carr and Galloway, though tried in due
course for the murder of Fielding and his son, were
acquitted, found to have been acting against their
wills and out of fear for their lives.

Now, as in 1844, the public has a strong fascination with pirates. Popular movies and books tell us
familiar stories of roguishly appealing swashbuck-
lers in pursuit of fantastic treasure. But cases like

that of the *Saladin* remind us that all too often pirates were simply brutal thugs, in whose wakes floated the battered corpses of their victims. No adventures were had, no treasures secured, no jolly times enjoyed—there was just the finality of death—for some at the head of an axe, for others at the end of a rope.

CHAPTER ELEVEN

Bill Johnston: Patriot Pirate of the Thousand Islands

Patriotism is the last refuge of a scoundrel.

–Samuel Johnson, compiler of the first
English dictionary

TODAY, MOST PEOPLE THINK OF THE THOUSAND ISLANDS AS a backdrop for summer cottages, curving white sails and broad, scudding clouds. But during the 1830s, these same islands were the stage for a series of political intrigues and piratical exploits. The far flung, rocky isles of Lake Ontario and the lower St. Lawrence River served as secret bases for the famous freshwater buccaneer Bill Johnston.

The story of Johnston's life reads like a pulp-fiction melodrama. Forever bent on revenge against the British, he never hesitated to put himself in danger's way. He waged his campaign from a series of concealed island caves, conducting raids in one area, then hiding for a couple of days in a secret lair before popping up somewhere completely different. On the run from Canadian and U.S. authorities, he became a popular folk hero who had allies on both sides of the border.

He captured the public's imagination by thumbing his nose at the British authorities and eluding capture for months at a time. When he *was* captured, no jail could hold him for long, and his escapes were as much the stuff of legend as his crimes.

In a further twist of melodrama, he was ably assisted by his intrepid daughter Kate, later dubbed "The Queen of the Thousand Islands." Their adventures were the subject of no less than two novels and a play (later described as possessing "little merit as works of literature and none at all as history"). It is difficult to separate the fact from the fiction of the Johnstons' lives. Bill was his own best publicist, and many of the tall tales associated with him come from a fabled family scrapbook, which disappeared sometime in the 1930s, never to be seen again. What we are left with is a smattering of fact, a healthy dose of scholarly speculation and a veritable broadside of wild conjecture—here it is.

Somewhere in The Thousand Islands (Summer 1838)

To local residents she was a familiar sight: a diminutive young woman in her late teens expertly rowing her little boat to and fro among the rocky, tree-tufted islands. They all knew perfectly well who she was: Kate Johnston, daughter of the famous fugitive Bill Johnston. It was an open secret that she regularly rowed out to her father's many hiding places to take him food and supplies. Sometimes, for company, her cousin Ada Randolph went with her, and to a stranger, this innocent picture of two young women in a boat held no hint of clandestine intrigue. Locals on both sides of the border knew differently, but so popular were Bill and his appealing daughter that nobody wanted to turn them in.

Kate was dark haired with a striking face, described as "noble," "handsome" and "lovely." By all accounts she excelled at both rowing and shooting, having been taught these necessary life skills by her father. During her father's many stints as a fugitive, she ferried food and information to him, all the while eluding watchful officials who fruitlessly attempted to follow her. She is alleged to have actively misinformed local authorities as to her father's whereabouts and intentions. She was a resourceful ally, a good friend and a loyal daughter.

Before the 1800s had ended, Kate Johnston's pluck, character and dedication to her father had captured the imagination of a Victorian culture obsessed with filial devotion. Even in the 1920s and '30s, publications in the Great Lakes area were still running stories about her indomitable spirit. Writing more than one hundred years later, "John Northman" (the likely pseudonym of a staff-writer at *The Canadian Magazine*) described her as having "a beauty and self reliance rarely equaled even in that land of virile womanhood."

And here begins the problem of separating fact from fiction regarding the Johnstons. While there are plenty of surviving newspaper articles from within their lifetimes, reporters during the 1800s rarely let the facts get in the way of a good story. Modern writers began using these earlier writers as sources, adding their own spin to already distorted events. Journalists like John Northman buried the facts under a thick layer of pulpy prose that was fun to read but didn't always make sense, hence the oxymoronic (and just plain moronic) phrase "virile womanhood." In most of these accounts, the basic facts are probably true, but the juicy details that readers enjoy latching on to are questionable.

Most frustrating, though, are the plausible tales that we *want* to be true. According to Northman, one day Kate was out in her little boat when two British officers approached in a small boat of their own. They stopped her and demanded that she take them to her father. Casually working her oars, Kate moved her own boat alongside, then deftly plucked a rifle from the bottom of her boat and trained it on the startled soldiers. She ordered them to tie the two boats together and row her to safety on the American side of the river, whereupon she let them go.

Although the day-to-day details of the Johnstons' lives are largely a matter of speculation and sometimes, outright fiction, the larger arc of their adventures are documented fact. The big events, after all, are the ones that count, and of those there is little doubt.

After the American Revolution ended in 1783, the Great Lakes provided an uneasy buffer between humbled English forces and the weary but proud Americans. Where exactly the border between the Canadas and the United States was remained somewhat unclear. The farmers and merchants who plied their trades along shores of the Great Lakes were far more concerned with commerce than with nationalism. Many residents did not consider themselves to be American or British, but rather, "Canadian." And many more simply couldn't be bothered to decide.

The War of 1812 changed all that. Although it was a conflict marked by undecided loyalties, the war polarized residents on both sides of the border. When the war ended in 1815, the only thing either side could be sure of was that they had gained a clear boundary line dividing the United States from Upper and Lower Canada. Now there was an increased interest in national politics, and if one was not American, then one was English or Canadian.

By the mid 1830s there was also a new group of players on the scene—the "Patriots." The self-titled Patriots were a group of mainly American rabble-rousers who advocated the "liberation" of Canada from British rule. Not surprising, most Canadians displayed resounding apathy towards "liberation," but this did not dampen the zeal of the Patriots. They were hungry for another separatist war with England, and support north of the new border came from a group of malcontent, British-born Canadians. The U.S. government officially disapproved of the Patriots' provocative aggression, but it was also inclined to give them a wide rein.

Enter Bill Johnston.

William Johnston was born in Trois-Rivières, Québec, on February 1, 1782. At the age of 16 he was apprenticed to a blacksmith. Blacksmithing was hot, hard, heavy work, and Johnston didn't much care for it. When his apprenticeship ended, he went to Kingston and there claims to have built his own boat, using it to haul freight across Lake Ontario.

In 1810 he married Ann Randolph of Washington County, New York. He would later jokingly write that when he married her, all of his other troubles seemed to begin: "With her came the attendant troubles in a great measure, of my subsequent life. In consequence of my alliance with the Yankees, as the people of these States were called by the Canadians, I was looked upon with a jealous eye by the more local subjects of His Most Gracious Majesty George III, and my acts were closely watched by the slaves of the despot." In reality, the marriage seems to have been a good one, weathering 50 years and innumerable trials and tribulations.

His "alliance with the Yankees" refers to the fact that he kept trading with American merchants, even though legislation, like the Non-Intercourse Act, made it illegal. While some mariners turned to privateering to replace lost revenue, other U.S. merchants often obtained secret licences from the British authorities, giving them safe passage through British-controlled waters. Many, including Bill Johnston, chose a third option: smuggling.

In 1811 he sold his boat and used the money to go into "the mercantile business." The *Kingston Chronicle and Gazette* ran the following advertisement in 1812:

Groceries for Sale
Cheap as the Cheapest, by the Subscriber

Rum	Barley Sugar
Nutmegs	Root and Ground Ginger
Shrub	Tobacco
Cloves	Allspice
Peppermint Cordial	Scotch Snuff
Peppermint Lozenges	Barley
Loaf and Muscovado Sugar	Segars [cigars], by the dozen or hundred
Confectionates	Oatmeal
Green Tea	Bottled Mustard
Liquorice	Rice
Coffee	Washing and Shaving Soap

–Wm. Johnston

But the British forces were still wary, and after
the War of 1812 broke out they kept an even closer
eye on Johnston. On November 10, 1812, Johnston was arrested on suspicion of slipping secrets
to the U.S. Navy. He protested his innocence:
"Up to this time I solemnly declare that I had no
communication with the American navy or army,
or any individual to my knowledge by whom any
information was likely to be conveyed to the
enemy, to the injury of His Majesty's subjects, or
those in his realm." After 12 hours he was let go
due to lack of evidence, but he was watched closely
during following weeks.

On June 1, 1813, Johnston was arrested again
and thrown into a Kingston jail. He quickly
escaped into the nearby woods, where he stum-
bled upon several Americans skulking around in
the trees to avoid capture by the British. Together,
they stole a birch bark canoe and paddled across
Lake Ontario but were soon picked up by a friendly
U.S. schooner that took them back to Sacket's Har-
bor in upstate New York.

Johnston was safe on U.S. soil, but he had been
forced to leave behind his business, his property
and his merchandise. What had previously been a
simmering dislike of the English was now fanned
into a burning flame of hatred. According to Johnston, his house, four acres of land and various
mercantile goods had been worth £30,000. Historians have assessed the actual value of Johnston's
lost property at closer to £1500, and so unless he

had a vast hoard of treasure buried somewhere, he outrageously exaggerated his own net worth. At any rate, his rage and frustration were real, and he later wrote, "I have suffered much from British tyranny. My property has been confiscated and my family beggared."

For the remainder of the war, Johnston put his knowledge of the St. Lawrence River to good use, becoming a spy-for-hire and general agitator on behalf of the U.S. His favourite stunt was to hijack the British mail coaches and turn their contents over to the American military. He was also good at handling small watercraft, and before U.S. General James Wilkinson's plan to capture Montréal ended at the Battle of Crysler's Farm, the man he'd hired to pilot his boat up the river was none other than William Johnston.

Jim Eagan is a retired New York State Trooper who spent the better part of a decade researching Johnston, sifting through old documents, scouring archives and visiting countless libraries in both the U.S. and Canada. He is the first to admit that when it comes to Pirate Bill, separating reality from wishful thinking is nearly impossible. Furthermore, he points out, much of accepted Johnston lore comes to us from a document that no longer seems to exist, namely the Johnston family scrapbook. It was probably a combination of press clippings and handwritten documents—all selected and preserved by the man himself. The scrapbook was cited in countless newspaper and magazine articles about Johnston, but it disappeared in 1932. We can only wonder at what the story of Bill Johnston would have been like as told by...Bill Johnston.

In the years after the war, Johnston settled in Clayton, New York, and set up shop again as a merchant. From Clayton, Johnston watched with interest as a vocal cadre of Upper Canadians began to turn against the so-called Family Compact. The "Compact" was an informal name for the influential group of wealthy families and Protestant clergy who dominated government in Upper Canada— much to the chagrin of those who were neither wealthy nor Protestant. In 1834, the Compact's most vocal opponent managed to get himself elected as the first mayor of Toronto. His name was William Lyon Mackenzie.

Mackenzie was about to become famous for his failed rebellion of 1837. When the coup flopped, Mackenzie fled to Buffalo, beaten in battle, but not in spirit. Since he was unable to find adequate numbers of Canadians who wanted to be liberated from the British, Mackenzie surrounded himself with *Americans* who wanted Canadians to be liberated from the British. Together, they called themselves the "Provisional Government of the Republic of Upper Canada." Their first official act was to go into hiding on Navy Island, a heavily wooded site on the Niagara River, about three miles above the falls.

Exactly what this location allowed them to govern, besides rocks and trees, is difficult to surmise. The island was a clever choice, however, in that it was under Canadian jurisdiction but only accessible from the American shore. Mackenzie could therefore have the satisfaction of knowing he was actually *in* the country he claimed to be leading. At the same time, no one was around to remind him that his only citizens were a thick forest of trees and an even thicker group of ne'er-do-wells from Buffalo.

To lead the fledgling state's army, Mackenzie chose a drunkard named Rensellaer van Rensellaer. Van Rensellaer decided that as well as an army, the Republic of Upper Canada should also have a navy. As luck would have it, someone introduced van Rensellaer to Johnston, describing him as "a gentleman of intelligence equal to fifty ordinary men" and capable of rallying "two hundred bold volunteers as ever drew a trigger." Finally, the man said, Johnston would be eager to "greatly annoy the Kingstonians." Johnston was certainly not inclined to argue with any of these modest claims. He graciously accepted his appointment as "Commodore of the Patriot Navy in the East."

The provisional government's American supporters used a steamboat, the *SS Caroline,* to ferry supplies out to them from the U.S. shore. The British quickly caught wind of this arrangement and put an end to it. On December 29, 1837, Andrew MacNabb and Royal Navy Captain Andrew Drew took a contingent of Canadian militia across the international boundary line and into U.S. waters. There, they seized control of the *Caroline* and in so doing killed an American named Amos Durfee. Next, they towed the *Caroline* out into the current, which dragged her inexorably towards the horseshoe-shaped cauldron at the end of the river. Finally, they set fire to the vessel, and she tilted over the falls to a destruction that was both fiery and wet.

Understandably, the death of Durfee and the destruction of the *Caroline* caused widespread outrage; during peacetime, Canadians had crossed into U.S. territory, killed a U.S. citizen and destroyed a U.S. vessel. It also spelled an end to the Provisional Government of the Republic of Upper Canada. Now cut off from their supply of food and information, the Patriots packed up camp and left for Kingston.

Unable to maintain a secret hideout on a small island, the Patriots next decided to invade Upper Canada. Kingston was the obvious target; its location was strategically crucial and it housed many important supply depots. For the Republic's new headquarters, Johnston chose two islands near the mouth of the St. Lawrence: Wellesley Island and Abel's Island. The rebels now had two secret strongholds, with Johnston's home in nearby Clayton as an auxiliary base.

The plan was as follows: On February 19, three bands of Patriots would break into American armouries in Watertown, Batavia and Elizabethtown. They would steal enough rifles and arms for a large invasion force. Over the following two days, Johnston and van Rensellaer would gather as many rebel sympathizers as they could. The men would encamp on Hickory Island so that the two fortified islands would remain secret. Then on February 22, the force would walk across the frozen river and take Kingston by storm. At least that was the plan.

The theft of the weapons was accomplished without incident, but after that things went down hill. To begin with, the freezing cold gales of February made it difficult to find large numbers of men willing to walk across a windswept, frozen river, much less camp out on a windswept, frozen island. What started out as a hot-headed force of 300 quickly dwindled to an icy-toed contingent of 35.

When a battalion of Canadian militia arrived at Hickory Island, all they found were less than three dozen demoralized, half-frozen men with no guns and a few bags of scrap metal to be used as grapeshot.

Johnston's Patriots went into hiding for the rest of the winter, but they were already hatching a new plot; if they could just steal a couple of steamboats this would give them a new way to ferry guns and food around on. They would have greater mobility, greater and greater strength—and surely the Republic of Canada would not be far behind.

WELLESLEY ISLAND, NEAR KINGSTON (MAY 29, 1838)
MCDONALD'S WHARF

Dock-hand Ripley looked across the late afternoon water to where the longboat had just appeared *again*. She was a trim little craft, and from where he stood, she looked to be about 30–40 feet long with one long pair of sweeps and five pairs of oars. Her white hull had a black stripe along the waterline with a jaunty yellow one around the gunwale, and sometimes Ripley caught the flash of a bright red interior. She looked to be carrying about 20 men: 12 at the oars and another 8 or so in front. The skipper was in the stern, sitting on a little raised section of deck and steering with an oar thrust into the water.

Wellesley Island was a regular refuelling stop for steamships travelling through the Thousand Islands. On the south shore was McDonald's Wharf, stacked with wood to feed the fires of shipboard boilers. Ripley was in charge of gathering the wood so that there was enough on hand when steamboats tied up to refuel. As he looked at the longboat out on the water, he found it rather odd that the men, all evidently good rowers, should be loitering near a rather isolated wharf with no apparent purpose. He had spotted them several times that day and had even seen some of them on the island when he was out collecting wood in the afternoon.

At around midnight, the dull slapping sound of a paddlewheel drifted across the water to Ripley's ears—a boat was coming. Abruptly, from the darkness of the nearby water, he also heard a man's voice say, "She is coming." It could only have been from one of the men in the boat, sitting and waiting for an approaching vessel to arrive.

As the steamboat drew closer, Ripley realized it was the *Sir Robert Peel,* and this got him thinking. The *Peel* was well known on the lake as a big, fast, fine ship, regularly hauling wealthy passengers to and fro, up and down Lake Ontario. One of her owners was Judge Jones from Brockville, a staunch loyalist who meted out harsh sentences when rebels turned up in his courtroom. If a group of Patriot rebels were to pick any ship on the lake as a target, it would be the *Peel.*

As soon as the *Peel* landed, Ripley approached her captain, John B. Armstrong. He told Armstrong of his well-founded suspicions. Armstrong laughed the idea off, saying that unless there were 100 or 150 men on the little vessel, he was not worried. After all, with 65 passengers on board and miscellaneous crew members, what could a group of 20 men do? Armstrong sent his men out to help Ripley gather wood.

On the other side of the island, Johnston's gang dressed and painted themselves as Indians. This would terrorize those aboard the *Peel* since they had all heard gory war stories of scalps peeled from tomahawk-shattered skulls. The men also armed themselves with pistols, swords and pikes eight feet long. Armed to the teeth, and now of fearful appearance, Johnston and his men set off through the woods towards the wharf on the other side of the island.

At about two in the morning they sprang out of the woods and descended on the slumbering ship. Johnston's raiders noisily battered down doors, broke windows and pried open hatches. One man guarded the gangway to stop the crew from boarding in case they returned. Six took over the engine room, and the rest herded Captain Armstrong and his frightened, bed-clothed passengers onto the deck. The pirates ignored pleas to allow the women and children to dress more warmly and openly laughed at the chivalrous souls who suggested that the ladies should be allowed to keep their jewellry. They addressed one another by code names, calling themselves Tecumseh, Davy Crockett, Nelson, Bolivar and Admiral Benbow. And throughout the proceedings were heard many cries of "Remember the *Caroline!*"

The pirates lost no time in putting their captives ashore. This done, they cut the mooring lines and inexpertly guided their new prize out into the open river. It should come as no surprise to anyone that piloting a 150-foot ship powered by steam is a lot different from piloting a longboat driven by 12 oars, but Johnston and his men didn't consider this. Although expert oarsmen, none of the men had any idea how to ignite the *Peel*'s boiler. The ship drifted for about 500 feet and then became stuck on a shoal.

Since they could not get her off the shoal, for the next 90 minutes the men loaded their spoils into five smaller boats. All things considered, they did well for themselves. The value of the money and jewellry was a healthy £20,000. We can only imagine Johnston's delight when he discovered that the ship was also carrying £15,000 worth of specie (coins), destined to pay British soldiers in Upper Canada.

Once they had transferred their considerable treasure, Johnston and his men set fire to the *Peel* in no less than five places. Then they boarded their plunder-laden dinghies and began pulling for their secret base on nearby Abel's Island. Johnston looked at his men's faces glowing warmly in the darkness, each one lit by the flames that were burning the *Sir Robert Peel* down to the watcr line.

A week later, on June 7, 1838, two parties of men went ashore on Amherst Island, near Kingston. Richard Bonnycastle, the British commandant of nearby Fort Henry, wrote that "Three isolated farmhouses were plundered, and many valuables and some money obtained; whilst one farmer, in defense of his property, was inhumanely shot at, and lost three fingers and a part of his hand. The pirates were dressed as sailors and well armed and it is said they had one sixteen-oared boat, mounting two three-pounders."

According to newspaper articles published more than one hundred years later, the first homestead hit was that of the prosperous Preston family. When the head of the household, Robert Preston, resisted, the pirates beat him with a pistol butt until he passed out. The man whose fingers were shot off appears to have been Preston's son, who was wounded when he tried to help his father; he lost so much blood that he died the next day. The pirates then kicked Mrs. Preston into unconsciousness and made off with $600 and two silver watches.

At about the same time, a second raiding party burst into the home of Isaac Patterson, where Mrs. Patterson was the only one at home. The robbers discovered a large locked chest that they made ready to smash open. But the quick-thinking Mrs. Patterson told them it contained only "dead clothes"—old clothes kept on hand to dress corpses in the event of a death. The pirates believed her and left the trunk—which in fact contained all the family cash and silver.

There is some question as to whether Johnston was actually present during these attacks. Some writers point to a level of viciousness that seems out of character, but others point out that he habitually went about armed with at least two pistols and a Bowie knife. Once, he had robbed a mail coach and beaten those who had challenged him. Another time he robbed a soldier and shot his horse. If he didn't actually participate in the

Amherst Island attacks, then the men were almost certainly acting under his orders.

While a good chunk of the citizenry on both sides of the border embraced Bill as one of their own, the governments of both Canada and the U.S. realized that they had a problem on their hands. Johnston himself also seems to have recognized that he would do well not to make everyone angry, and shortly after the Amherst Island raids he published a declaration in U.S. newspapers. In part, it read:

> *I, William Johnston, a native-born citizen of Upper Canada, certify that I hold a commission in the Patriot Service of Upper Canada as Commander in Chief of the naval force and flotilla. I commanded the expedition that captured and destroyed the steamer,* Sir Robert Peel. *The men under my command in that expedition were nearly all natural born English subjects.... The object of my movement is the independence of the Canadas. I am not at war with the commerce or property of the people of the United States.*

Finding a handful of men in the Thousand Islands is no easy proposition, especially when they don't want to be found. Colonel Charles Grey later wrote, "These islands are perfectly beautiful, but a place so formed for a buccaneer I never saw. Johnston has only to keep quiet for a certain time and it is impossible to find him...I hear he is very popular even with those who do not join him...It seems absurd that one man should keep a whole country in hot water but so it is."

Johnston enjoyed the shelter of several different islands during the time he was a fugitive. Whichever island hideaway he happened to be at was dubbed "Fort Wallace." Popular legend has it that Johnston's island lairs were caves with entrances hidden by crooked trees. Through gaps in the rock the tireless Kate would slide him food on the end of a wooden board. Again, this is popular legend: Why she should slide food to him on a board instead of just walking in and giving it to him remains unclear.

The largest of these caves was rumoured to be 100 feet long and 20 feet wide. It was so large that Johnston and his men are said to have put up partitions, dividing it into separate rooms. They built beds from pine planks, used sawhorses to support crude tables, made seats out of wooden packing crates and built a fireplace under an opening in the ceiling. Again, "rumour" is the operative word here.

The island most often associated with Johnston is Devil's Oven. It has been claimed that this was Johnston's favourite hiding spot, but this does not seem likely. Devil's Oven is a little tea biscuit of rock plopped down into the waters of the St. Lawrence. It is quite close to its neighbouring islands and clearly visible from all of them. Aside from a tuft of trees on the top and some scraggly growth around the shore, there are not many places to hide. At most it would have made a good rendezvous spot for Bill and Kate.

Whatever purpose Johnston may have put it to, Devil's Oven has spawned more half-baked stories than any of his other supposed hideouts.

According to one legend, one day Johnston was enjoying his after-breakfast pipe when there appeared at the mouth of his cave a little group of British soldiers led by Captain George Walker Boyd. At gunpoint they ordered Johnston to stand down. He casually took the pipe out of his mouth and held it over a nearby barrel of something that looked suspiciously like gunpowder. Unless they let him be, Johnston threatened to tip the embers of his pipe into the barrel and blow them all up! The soldiers scrambled over themselves in their haste to get away, and Johnston went back to smoking his pipe.

In most versions of the story, the final punch line is that the barrel was really full of (wait for it)... onion seeds. We are left to wonder what possible purpose a man on the run from the law could have for carting a barrel of onion seeds around with him, unless perhaps it was in style at the time.

Having failed to "liberate" Canada twice, the Patriot forces decided to try for a third time. The plan was that three ships full of raiders would dock at Prescott, Ontario, and stage a surprise attack on nearby Fort Wellington. Starting on November 11, the first part of the plot went according to plan, and three ships loaded with several hundred paid enlistees set out from the American side. Johnston, as "Commodore," took command of one of the ships, *The Charlotte of Oswego*. What followed was a repeat of the *Sir Robert Peel* fiasco; Johnston ran his ship aground. This time it wasn't a rocky shoal that caught her up but a natural embankment of mud on the bottom of the river. Two other ships repeatedly tried to pull the *Charlotte* off the sludgy obstacle, but to no avail. Before long, a British steamer, the *Experiment,* appeared and opened fire not only on the *Charlotte* but also the ships trying to help her.

As night fell, Johnston took 30 men, and a large quantity of ammunition, and quit the venture altogether. A witness later testified that he swore to return and destroy the *Experiment,* which he referred to as "that damned little boat." However, once back on the U.S. side of the border, he did nothing more than bluster about and encourage others to fight for the glory of a republican Canada.

With one of their ships run aground, and her commander gone, the rebels hastily abandoned their original plan and came up with a new one. They landed at Prescott, went ashore and took over a windmill, where they holed up for four days, before the British drove them out. About 16 British were killed, with no reliable record of Patriot losses. The battered men in the windmill were rounded up, put on trial and their leaders hanged.

Johnston had got clear away once more, but not for long.

By this time, the "Pirate of the Thousand Islands" was not only well known but also had a price on his head. After the destruction of the *Peel*, capturing Bill Johnston was worth a cool $500 to whoever could bring him in. It says something about his personal popularity that even though he consorted with thieves, smugglers, pirates and rebels, none of them ever turned him in for the reward. In the end, it was U.S. forces that caught Johnston on November 17, 1838.

His "trial," if one can call it that, was by all accounts incredibly casual, and eventually he was released due to an alleged lack of evidence. But the man who had been chasing him for all these months, a U.S. marshal named Garrow, wasn't about to let him get away. Garrow re-arrested Johnston and threw him in jail, from whence he escaped before spending even a single night there.

Johnston was a long way from the Thousand Islands at this point, and he seems to have realized that eventual capture was inevitable. Hearing that his arrest was worth $500, he reasoned that if someone was going to get the money, it might as well be one of his own children. Preliminary arrangements were made for him to surrender his weapons to his son, John. But soon they both heard that Bill would be held without bail, and the elder Johnston went back into hiding. He was finally caught in a small cabin in upstate New York on December 10, 1838. Turning to the arresting officer, he simply said, "It is well you came tonight for you would not have found me tomorrow."

At his trial, Johnston denied having anything to do with the attack on Prescott and said that he had never been in favour of the attack, but rather, had tried to persuade the instigators that they could never hope to succeed with such a poorly organized force. In the end, he was sentenced to one year in jail and fined $250.

Johnston began serving his time, but it wasn't much of a confinement. For one thing he was quickly allowed to walk about the streets of Albany on parole. And it wasn't long before the ever faithful Kate turned up, voluntarily coming to stay either in the jail itself or nearby, so she could keep her father company. Bill Johnston also appears to have staged a benefit for himself, on January 23, 1839. The promised entertainment was a performance of a play called "Bill Johnston, the Hero of the Great Lakes." The notice in the newspaper went on to say, "Bill Johnston and his Daughter will be present. It is hoped his friends will make their appearance, and use their influence to assist him on this occasion." It was pretty harsh, this prison life.

After serving about six months of his sentence, Johnston escaped again. He allegedly secured a pardon signed by William Henry Harrison, who was about to die his way into the record books as the U.S. president who sat the shortest term (30 days, 11 hours, 30 minutes). Johnston was now

57, and the rough-and-tumble life of pirating was becoming a bit much. He managed to get himself appointed as a lighthousekeeper in Clayton, then became an innkeeper, and some say returned to his former profession of smuggling.

He was visited often in these later years, and travellers were excited to meet the man who had wrought havoc from one side of the border to the other. Someone once asked Johnston what good all of his exploits had done. He conceded that his adventures had been but stumbling blocks in history's path. He did, however, maintain that he had caused the British a lot of trouble, saying, "Do you call the expenditure of four millions of British cash nothing? That is what our side has gained."

He led a much quieter life for the remainder of his days and died on February 17, 1870, at the age of 88. Kate followed him just seven years later, passing away in March 1878 at the age of 59.

What then is Johnston's legacy? Canada, the country he had fought so hard and so long to "liberate," became the Dominion of Canada, three years before he died. His views on this are not known. Kate and her eight or nine siblings left many descendants, some of whom are not even aware of their famous ancestor's adventures. In a glass case at the Clayton Historical Society in upstate New York is a silk apron that had been seized from a passenger on the *Sir Robert Peel* and given as a gift by Bill to his ever faithful daughter Kate.

Many would argue that the idea of their relationship is the real treasure to be found in this tale; a parent and child who recognized themselves in one another and liked what they saw. In our imaginations, the two will always be bobbing in a little boat, just far enough off shore to be out of range of musket balls, one rowing earnestly, the other thumbing his nose at the people on the shore.

CHAPTER TWELVE

Brain Problems:
John Clibbon Brain,
Confederate Pirateer

*If I fail, it will be for lack of ability,
and not of purpose.*

—Abraham Lincoln

THE ONLY WORD TO DESCRIBE JOHN CLIBBON BRAIN IS
"pirateer"; that is, not quite a pirate and not quite
a privateer. During the American Civil War he
embarked on numerous expeditions and intrigues
for the southern cause. Sometimes his adventures
were successes, but other times they were failures
since his ambitions tended to outpace his abilities.
In one of his most well-known exploits, Brain
came to St. John, New Brunswick, and recruited a
crew of locals to first capture and then man a Confederate privateer against the overlords of the
Northern Union. In what became known as "The
Chesapeake Affair," the first part of his plan actually succeeded.

THE STEAMSHIP *CHESAPEAKE*, 20 MILES NORTHEAST OF CAPE COD (DECEMBER 7, 1863), BETWEEN 1:00 AND 2:00 AM

The engine of the *Chesapeake* chugged away rhythmically. In the engine room, Patrick Connor shovelled some more coal onto the fire and wiped the sweat from his forehead—it was hot in there. The *Chesapeake*'s three masts could carry sail, but her main means of getting about was a propeller driven by a steam engine. The engine's steam came from water vaporized by a fire that had to be kept burning evenly to create an adequate amount of heat. Connor was the *Chesapeake*'s fireman. He didn't put out fires, but instead, fuelled them, stoked them and made sure that they burned hot and even.

All through the night Connor stayed near the engine room, shovelling on more coal when the flames fell. Above him, the *Chesapeake*'s 22 passengers were asleep in their berths (or so he thought). Fore and aft of the engine room, the *Chesapeake*'s holds were silent and dark, packed with a cargo of flour, sugar, wine and leather. Unless either of the two engineers dropped by to adjust the controls of the engine, these were quiet hours.

Suddenly, however, without any warning, four men armed with pistols burst into the engine room and squeezed off several shots. Connor was so close that he came away with flash burns on his face and neck but miraculously was not wounded. He watched in horror as Second Engineer Odin

Shaffer burst through the door only to be hit by one of many bullets directed his way. Shaffer tried to scramble away but collapsed near the door.

Meanwhile, Chief Mate Charles Johnson was in his cabin, trying to stay awake with a cup of coffee. As soon as heard the shots ring out, he ran to the engine room and was immediately fired upon, though not hit. He fled, but two of the attackers gave chase. As Johnson approached the spot where Shaffer's body was heaped on the deck, the two men chasing him were joined by three other assailants. This new trio of men burst out of their hiding spot in the pilot house and opened fire, wounding Johnson in the elbow and knee. He limped onwards, determined to rouse the captain to tell him what was happening.

While Charles Johnson shuffled away into the darkness, Chief Engineer James Johnson (no relation) also hurried past the spot where Shaffer lay. As soon as he reached the engine room Engineer Johnson felt the barrel of a pistol pressed to his forehead and reflexively brought his arm up to knock the gunman's hand away. One of the other men in the room fired and the bullet lodged in the engineer's jaw but didn't kill him. Still conscious but now seriously wounded, James Johnson managed to scramble away into the covering safety of the darkness out on deck.

Elsewhere on the ship, the other wounded Johnson, Chief Mate Charles, had managed to reach Captain Isaac Willet's cabin and woke him up. Stepping out of his cabin door, Captain Willet later estimated that he was fired upon at least nine times, all of the shots missing. As he ran over and stooped to look at Shaffer, two more bullets whizzed past him. Whoever the assailants were, they seemed to like shooting, even if they weren't very good at it. Ducking several more shots, all of which also missed him, Willet was crouched near Shaffer when a man emerged and pointed a pistol at the captain's head. The man informed Willet that he was now a prisoner of the Confederate States of America and clapped a pair of handcuffs on him. Then Willet was taken to the main cabin, where he found the rest of the captives being held—all of them scared.

Out on deck, the two wounded Johnsons had met up, and now, leaning on each other for support, they made their way to the kitchen, just in time to hear the leader of the marauders tell three of his minions to toss Shaffer's body overboard. Seeing that resistance was futile, the two Johnsons surrendered and were taken to the main cabin, where they saw the captain and the rest of the captives. Out of 22 passengers, 16 had been part of the plot. The *Chesapeake* had fallen!

The leader of this band of Confederate raiders was John Clibbon Brain. He was born in Britain but his family moved to Ohio in the 1850s. It was

1861 when the civil war broke out, by which time Brain was training to be a gunner in the Southern army. After a stint in the Confederate Navy, he joined the Confederate Secret Service, rising to the rank of lieutenant. Undercover, he worked his way north of the Mason Dixon line posing as an illustrator who was making sketches for a railway guide. All the while, he was making drawings and gathering information about the enemy territory that could be useful to Confederate forces. He was caught but escaped by promising to go to Canada. In Montréal and Québec City, he earned money by selling subscriptions to a nonexistent "Grand Trunk Railway Guide." He must have been a good liar, because he earned enough to buy passage back to England, where he continued fraudulently selling railway guide subscriptions until he was caught again and shipped back to the U.S.

Back in the U.S., Brain ran into an old acquaintance from the Confederate Navy: Lieutenant Henry A. Parr, originally from Canada West (the old name for Upper Canada, more or less present-day Ontario). Somehow these two disgruntled Confederates joined forces with Vernon Guy Locke (alias John Parker). At the outbreak of the civil war, Locke had bought a beat-up old boat and converted it into a privateer. He rechristened his new ship *Retribution* and got a letter of marque in her name from Confederate Secretary of State Judah Benjamin. When Locke abandoned the *Retribution* in the Bahamas, he kept the letter of marque.

Brain, Parr and Locke hatched a daring, if dastardly, scheme. They would hijack a boat, rename her *Retribution* and use the old letter of marque as a licence to plunder Union shipping. The main thing wrong with this plot was that letters of marque only applied to the vessel they were issued for; they were nontransferable. Giving another vessel the same name didn't make it any more legal. Clearly though, law was not a going concern for the three men.

Now all they had to do was muster a crew with which to capture their soon-to-be ill-gotten prize. Where were they going to find a band of men both willingly to risk their lives for the promise of money and also sympathetic to the Confederate cause? Why, in New Brunswick of course!

Back then, this notion wasn't as daffy as it might seem today. Britain and Canada (as a British possession) were officially neutral, but both held a great deal for sympathy for the Confederacy. Many believed that the North was exercising unfair economic domination over the South. To Canadian abolitionists who professed the war to be primarily a struggle against slavery, others could counter with Lincoln's famous quote: "If I could save the Union without freeing any slave I would do it, and if I could save it by freeing all the slaves I would do it; and if I could save it by freeing some and leaving others alone I would also do that."

At the beginning of the civil war, tensions had nearly boiled over when a U.S. ship seized a British vessel and took two Confederate diplomats into custody. It was a well-known fact that U.S. Secretary of State William Seward wanted the U.S. to seize control of Britain's remaining North American possessions, namely Canada. The British army had even shipped in large numbers of troops to defend the border in case of an invasion. And so, as the war progressed, although neither Canada nor Britain recognized the Confederacy diplomatically, both continued doing business with southern interests and even built ships for the Confederate navy.

Pro-South sympathies in Canada were also fanned by the Union tactic of sending illegal army recruiters, called "crimpers," into Canadian colonies. Crimpers received a fee for every man they could sign up. In theory, the recruits were supposed to come voluntarily, but just as often they signed up while they were drunk, and on other occasions were brutally beaten to extract their signatures. Crimping became such a pressing issue that future first Prime Minister John A. Macdonald organized a force of special agents to entrap the illegal recruiters.

All of this meant that Confederate agitators could expect to find many a sympathetic ear in Canada. And that is exactly what Brain, Parr and Locke proceeded to do. In the back streets of St. John they held recruiting meetings where they offered lucrative rewards for those willing to join them. Privateers in their expedition would receive free passage to New York, a share in all prizes captured, a pistol plus ammunition and a bonus of $500 if their captured ship could penetrate the Union's naval blockade and make it as far as Washington.

It was a tall order. By this time the Yankee naval blockade effectively cut off the southern ports and firmly protected northern ones. And since Locke's letter of marque was for a ship he no longer owned, the whole operation was illegal under international law anyway. But the citizens of St. John didn't know that, and soon the trio of conspirators found 11 New Brunswickers to help them capture a ship: David Collins, George Robinson, Linus Seely, James McKinley, George Wade, H.C. Brooks, Robert Clifford and two sets of brothers: Gilbert and Robert Cox, as well as Moore and Isaac Treadwell.

Back on the *Chesapeake*, after taking over the ship, the privateers realized they had a problem: none of them knew how to run a steam engine. Keeping a steam engine running smoothly was far more complicated than just stoking a fire. There was a bewildering assortment of valves and gauges and knobs, each one controlling a fractional but crucial aspect of the engine's functioning. To his credit, Brain had recruited two engineers in New York the night before they sailed, but the pair had gotten so drunk that Brain wasn't able to get them on board the next morning.

Having killed Second Engineer Odin Shaffer, the privateers now turned to the wounded Chief Engineer James Johnson. Even with a bullet in his chin, Johnson was somehow able to function and kept the *Chesapeake*'s engine running smoothly. The privateers also realized that none of them knew how to navigate, and they forced one of the passengers, former ship's captain Robert Osborne, to pilot their stolen vessel into Grand Manan, New Brunswick.

At Grand Manan, they went ashore and picked up Locke and another man who had joined the crew. Then, the *Retribution,* as they now called her, sailed on to St. John, where the privateers loaded their captives into the ship's pilot boat and cut her loose. It was about three miles to shore, and while the *Retribution* steamed off, her rightful crew hastily rowed ashore and told the local authorities what had happened. From St. John, telegraph wires quickly relayed the news of the *Chesapeake*'s capture to ports up and down the east coast. In a matter of minutes she had become a wanted ship.

Brain and his crew of privateers were now running short of money. Aside from having an invalid letter of marque, their next actions show that they were rank amateurs as far as privateering went. They "broke bulk"; that is, they cracked open the cargo holds and started selling off $80,000 worth of goods piecemeal. In an ideal world, cargo captured by privateers was supposed to be taken back to port and sold at auction. Privateers who "broke bulk" immediately became subject to piracy charges, and any profits they might have realized from the legitimate auction of their cargo were forfeit.

As Brain and his cohorts steamed through the Maritimes they were welcomed with open arms. At Yarmouth, La Have, Shelburne, Petite Riviere and St. Mary's Bay, local residents were overjoyed that the resourceful Confederates had made such an audacious capture; it was a gratifying humiliation of the arrogant Unionists. On December 10, 1863, the *Halifax Morning Chronicle* summed up the general glow of good feeling: "Southern daring has just added another feat to its list of astonishing achievements." Of course, it couldn't have hurt either that wherever the *Chesapeake* (now the *Retribution*) put into port, her crew came ashore offering flour, sugar, wine and leather at bargain prices.

But by this time, the *Retribution* had grown a tail—the *Ella & Annie*, commanded by Lieutenant Nicholls of the U.S. Navy, dogged the *Retribution*'s every step. Near Lunenberg, the errant Confederates just managed to get out of Nicholls' clutches. And only a postmistress sympathetic to the privateers prevented Nicholls from capturing Parr when both men had gone to the same telegraph office within a few minutes of each other. Later, the American vice-consul in Nova Scotia said that local residents had actually hampered efforts to catch the fugitives.

On December 13 though, the *Retribution*'s luck finally ran out. She was cruising alongside the *Investigator*, a small vessel sent from Halifax by Locke to replenish the *Retribution*'s coal supply. The *Investigator* was commanded by Captain Holt, and as well as coal, she also carried two brothers, William and Alexander Henry—the two engineers Brain had hired in New York but who were too hungover to report for duty the day their ship sailed. Suddenly the *Ella & Annie* appeared, steaming steadily towards the privateers. On board the *Retribution*, pandemonium broke out as the privateers scrambled to abandon ship, knowing they were cornered. They left their breakfast sitting on the table, along with the two Henry brothers who were asleep on the *Investigator*.

Lieutenant Nicholls came on board and, with a drawn pistol, hunted around for the fugitives. Empty-handed, he next boarded the *Investigator* and promptly arrested the brothers Henry as well as George Wade, one of the actual privateers. Nicholls treated them so roughly and stormed about with such a belligerent manner that Captain Holt objected, whereupon Nicholls threatened to put him in irons and take him to Boston. With his three prisoners and the *Retribution*, Captain Nicholls steamed back towards Boston. But on the way he crossed paths with another U.S. ship, the *Dacotah*, commanded by Captain A.G. Clary. Captain Clary realized that Lieutenant Nicholls had committed what amounted to an act of piracy: He had arrested a British subject (George Wade) at gunpoint in British waters as well as detaining and threatening Captain Holt, who was from Halifax. Hoping to avoid an international incident, Clary turned the whole expedition around and headed to Halifax, hoping that if he openly reported what had happened and let the British authorities handle the case, things wouldn't boil over.

Upon their arrival in Halifax, it was immediately discovered that this dashing Confederate escapade had actually resulted in the death of an innocent man, Odin Shaffer. Gone were the fawning words of the pro-South newspapers. Now they indignantly voiced their outrage. The Union papers got into the act too, muttering darkly of treacherous sabotage perpetrated by British subjects (by whom they meant Brain and his colleagues). Frustratingly, other than the two Henry brothers, there was no one to stand trial since the ringleaders had gotten clean away when the *Ella & Annie* appeared. Everyone disowned Brain; the Confederates said he wasn't really a Confederate since his letter of marque was invalid—that just made him a pirate, and obviously an English one. And the British said Brain was clearly an American of some sort because he had been living there for at least 11 years. But really, it was all academic, since Brain was nowhere to be seen.

After much contentious legal wrangling, the *Chesapeake* was returned to her rightful owners. And after laying low for a while, Brain and three of his men slipped back into St. John, where they were promptly arrested. Bizarrely though, Brain was released, and his three companions never stood trial either. The reasons for these surprising outcomes were complicated, all related to whether Brain and his men were operating under legitimate orders from the Confederate government; whether the deck of a U.S. ship in British waters constituted U.S. jurisdiction and which kinds of courts could rule on which kinds of cases. In the end, Brain and his friends went free, while neither the Canadian, Union, Confederate, nor British interests were satisfied. Needless to say, relations between the Union and the Maritime provinces were not improved by this incident.

But Brain's Canadian exploits were not quite over yet. Proceeding to Lake Erie, he and his cohorts took over a little steamer, hoisted a Confederate flag and captured several vessels. Their adventures came to an end when they deliberately ran the steamer aground and set fire to her. After this Brain made his way home to the shattered southern states, and from this point on, he fades from history.

The *Chesapeake* Affair puts a spotlight on unexpected Canadian loyalties. Nowadays, we like to think of ourselves as a progressive, tolerant society. But nothing would seem further from that ideal than aiding and abetting operatives of the slave-driving Confederate states. To make sense of this, it helps to remember that the U.S. was just about 90 years old, and Canada didn't even exist yet as a nation. To some extent, "Canadians" thought of themselves as "British." And as good "Britons," they remained suspicious of the upstart nation to the south that had broken away from the Crown less than one hundred years previous.

There was a deeply rooted suspicion that the government in Washington was planning to take over Canada, and indeed many U.S. politicos vocally advocated such a course of action. With the outbreak of the civil war came a mixture of relief and sympathy: relief that Washington would be too tied up with the South to bother trying to take over Canada, and sympathy for the Confederacy, who many perceived to be bravely opposing the arrogance of Washington. Rooting for the underdog is something of a Canadian tradition, but one that led our ancestors to make choices we can scarcely believe today.

CHAPTER THIRTEEN

Gunpowder Gertie:
Pirate Queen of the Kootenays

*...we had a hope that if we lived and were good,
God would permit us to be pirates.*

–Mark Twain

WHEN THINGS ARE GOING WELL, ALL OF US FEEL LIKE PIRATES—
captains of our own destinies, riding the winds of
fortune, forging our own fates. And when things
aren't going well, the way of the pirate reminds us
that even when life seems to have left you
becalmed—stuck in the doldrums of daily routine—
at any moment a sail may appear over the horizon,
bringing with it riches and adventure. Since the late
1800s popular culture has painted the pirate life-
style as one to aspire to, full of carefree vagabond
wealth and swashbuckling good times.

Although in our minds most of us know these
assumptions to be untrue, in our hearts we need
to believe that it might all be possible. This need to
believe has led many people to jump to conclusions
based on faith instead of facts. In some cases, hunters of romance and seekers of treasure have made
life-changing decisions based on little more than
dreams and fancies.

One such story is that of Gunpowder Gertie, Pirate Queen of the Kootenays. Gertie's heyday was from 1898 to 1903. During these five short years she turned BC's Kootenay river system into her own private hunting ground. Her steamboat, the *Tyrant Queen*, had originally been built for the BC Provincial Police, and one enduring mystery is how she managed to steal this 42-foot vessel from a flatbed railway car in the dead of night. With a water-cooled Gatling gun mounted to her deck, the *Queen* made a formidable pirate cruiser, and Gertie set off on a series of exploits that soon became the stuff of legend. The story of how Gunpowder Gertie came to be a pirate illustrates the impact that tall tales can have on impressionable minds.

Most of what we know about Gertie comes from the research of her chief biographer, Carolyn McTaggart, a writer and educator living in Crescent Valley, BC. It was Ms. McTaggart who first brought to light contemporary newspaper accounts of Gertie's adventures, and the following excerpts are taken from one of Ms. McTaggart's many articles summarizing the life and times of this larger-than-life character.

> *Gertrude Imogen Stubbs was born in 1879, in Whitby, England, the daughter of George Stubbs, a train engineer and his wife, Violet, a seamstress. Whitby was a port town on the east coast of Britain and saw much ocean-going traffic, including the famous Captain Cook.*

Gertrude was a bit of a wild thing from the first; she liked nothing better than to spend her time down at the busy docks, eagerly listening to the stories of sea captains in port between voyages, or riding with her father on his route from Whitby to Pickering and Scarborough. Gertrude's family emigrated to Sandon, B.C. Canada in 1895 when her father accepted a job to run trains for the newly completed K&S Railway.

~

Less than a month after they had arrived in the thriving town of Sandon, Gertie's mother was tragically killed in an avalanche that destroyed their home on the steep mountainside at the north end of town. Gertie was coming home from her job at a general store in town and witnessed the whole thing. Her heartbroken father blamed himself for Violet's death and sank into drinking and gambling, leaving his only child pretty much to fend for herself. Gertie had to make sure her father actually made it for his shifts and accompanied him on his routes to Kaslo, helping him shovel coal. Finally, as he slid further into debt and depression, she was pretty much doing the actual running of the engine herself to enable her constantly drunken father to keep his job so they would not starve. After his death in 1896, the Railway refused to allow her to continue working for them because their policies did not include hiring women.

*Stranded in Kaslo without a penny after pay-
ing off her father's debts, she found what honest
work she could as a woman paid only starveling
wages. After barely eking out a living through the
winter, she cut her hair off short, disguised herself
as a young man and hired on as a coal hand on
the sternwheelers [a kind of steamboat common at
this time]. There she was happy and her knowledge of steam engines soon proved so useful that
she was given more responsibilities. Unfortunately,
Gertie's disguise was finally discovered. Her ship
and another were racing to establish which vessel
had the superior speed when the boiler ran dry.
The explosion in the engine room blinded her in
her right eye and knocked her unconscious. Gertie
was taken to the hospital where the attending doctor realized she was a woman. Without even com-
pensation for her injury she was given the sack,
nor would any other steam company hire her
on—nobody hired women.*

Furious and frustrated, Gertie was desperate to
find an outlet for her abilities. Her mind went back
to her life in Whitby. As a little girl she had spent
many happy hours listening to the stories of her
grandfather, who was a retired fisherman. She
would sit by, "with her chin in her hands, while
her grandfather and his cronies recounted grand
tales of the past—pirates, scourge of the Caribbean, naval battles, raids on rich foreign ports,
trading explorations, the circumnavigation of the
globe, exploration of exotic countries."

When she had discovered that Grandfather would not be coming to Canada with her and her parents, she was heartbroken. Seeing her disappointment, the old man gave his granddaughter something to remember him by. It was a child's toy common enough at the time—a little tin boat that made real steam from the heat of a candle. Plopped into a sink or a pond, it would bubble merrily to and fro until the candle burnt out. Knowing that Gertie was especially fascinated by tales of pirates, her grandfather had painstakingly made a little felt skull and crossbones flag that was mounted to a mast set into the bow. Across the stern he had also painted a name in miniature letters: *Tyrant Queen*.

Now this little toy was the only remaining artifact of a life that seemed very far away—one in which there were people who cared about her, or at the very least, people for *her* to care about. Turning the little tin boat over in her fingers, an outrageous idea began to form in her mind. And so was born Gunpowder Gertie, sprung from little more than an old man's recollections and a toy boat.

The *Tyrant Queen* started life as the *Witch*, a state-of-the-art steam cruiser that the area police had brought in to patrol the web of waterways that makes up the Kootenay river system. They made several modifications to the *Witch*: her hull was sheathed in steel and she was driven by two of the first ever "ducted" propellers. Today, ducted propellers are used more in aviation than marine travel, but back then they were touted as the next big thing. The propellers are encased in metal tubes or "ducts," which are only half-submerged in the water. Strange as it sounds, this actually improves their efficiency, and more of the energy that turns the propeller can be used to drive the boat. With a top speed of 22 knots, the *Witch* was the fastest ship on the waters. On the night of February 12, 1898, the *Witch* was resting in the railway yards, still on the flatbed rail car that had brought her to Nelson, BC. The next morning, however, the night guard was found unconscious, and the *Witch* was gone.

Steering her own course at last, Gertie became a pirate. With a band of followers she steamed her new ship, the *Tyrant Queen*, the length and breadth of the Kootenays, relieving passengers of their possessions and releasing the captive contents of shipboard safes. Typically, Gertie would pull alongside another boat while one of her crew trained the Gatling gun on their prey. Once the vessel had stopped, she would go on board, rob the passengers at pistol point, take any valuable cargo that might be in the hold, then leap back on the *Queen*, whereupon the whole party would disappear as fast as they had come.

She once robbed a charity cruise but turned nearly all of the proceeds over to the cause when she found out what she had done. She is reputed to have robbed no less an august personage than Oscar Wilde when he visited Kaslo, BC, in 1899.

She stole jewels, pilfered payrolls and hoarded cash. After paying off her crew and keeping the *Queen* in coal, it is not known how Gertie spent her ill-gotten gains.

Gertie's reign might have continued indefinitely had she not been betrayed by one of her own men. Bill Henson was an engine man who regularly expressed dissatisfaction with his share of the takings. In 1903 he struck a deal with the BC Provincial Police; in return for a handsome reward and a promise of clemency, he would help them to capture his boss. Henson gave Gertie a phony tip about a huge payroll shipment that was supposed to be coming into Kaslo on the *SS Moyie*.

Gertie ambushed the *Moyie* near what is now known as Redfish Creek, but she was in for a rude surprise. Instead of a carrying a payroll it was full of lawmen who were armed to the teeth. Knowing she was outgunned, Gertie stoked up the boiler and prepared to make her escape. The devious Henson, however, had sabotaged one of the gaskets, and as soon as the steam pressure reached full, the gasket blew. The crippled *Queen* was now a sitting duck, and a ferocious battle ensued. Gunpowder Gertie put up an enormous fight and local legend says that the river literally ran red with blood before the lawmen were able to board the *Queen* and clap her captain in irons.

Here, Carolyn McTaggart concludes the story of Gertie's adventures.

Gunpowder Gertie was sentenced to life imprisonment, but died of pneumonia during the terrible winter of 1912. She never revealed where she had hidden her ill-gotten gains. Rumour has it that she buried it somewhere along the river system she'd plundered and left a hidden map that would lead to the treasure. As all her crew perished in the final battle (including the turncoat Henson, who Gertie shot in the back when she spotted him trying to jump ship during the fray) she took her secret to the grave and to this day, no one has yet discovered the resting place of Gunpowder Gertie's gold.

It was 1995 when Carolyn McTaggart first told her class of grade three students about her discoveries regarding Canada's only female pirate. She showed them photocopies of some old newspaper articles, and her students excitedly went home and told their parents. Not surprisingly, the story of Gertie's adventures caught the interest of the local press, and in May 1995, a small local newsletter, the *Kootenay Review* ran the story. Interest was running high.

A couple of years later, a friend of Carolyn's called to say that the CBC radio program *This Day in History* had just run a piece on Gunpowder Gertie and her many adventures. It wasn't surprising really; a Canadian pirate and a spunky female one to boot? It was the kind of Canadian content that CBC producers lie awake at night dreaming about. Today, if you do a web search for "Gunpowder Gertie," you will see a plethora of websites all solemnly reciting the facts of her life, as far as they are known—in spite of the fact that *Gunpowder Gertie never existed.*

Ever since she was a little girl, Carolyn McTaggart had been fascinated by pirates. Her father had even built her a sturdy little wooden chest to fill with the treasures of her imagination. As an adult she came to have an abiding interest in the late 1890s because those years were the zenith of Victorian achievement in technology and exploration—there were steam engines, telegraphs and, in BC, the gold rush!

One night she was at a party when someone commented that the Mississippi River had had pirates, and even though the Kootenays didn't have any, they damn well should have. With all that gold and money floating around, an enterprising pirate could have gotten quite a fortune. This got her thinking: She knew that the shape of Kootenay Lake, combined with the surrounding river system, would have made good waters for a pirate to hide in.

Around this time, the class Carolyn was teaching had begun a unit on pirates. What if she invented an imaginary pirate as a way to make local history more exciting to her students? Before she'd left the party, Gunpowder Gertie had sprung into her imagination, fully formed.

The next step was to make it all seem believable. Carolyn set about fabricating false documents that would support the notion of a late 19th-century female river pirate. She found some old newspaper articles about local events and photocopied them. Next, she used computer fonts to match the typeface of the newspaper and wrote a few paragraphs about the exploits of Gunpowder Gertie. Then she pasted the paragraphs over sections of the newspaper articles, photocopied everything again, and voila—she had copies of what appeared to be authentic period newspaper articles.

Carolyn showed the different documents to her students and announced that Gertie had also left behind a treasure map, which Carolyn now produced. Following the clues of the treasure map, her students dug up a chest buried nearby and inside they found—gold coins!—which on closer examination proved to be delicious chocolate wrapped in gold foil.

The treasure may not have been real gold, but for the kids it was just as good. Then Ms. McTaggart revealed that Gertie herself was a fictional character, but that of course, the backdrop to her adventures, the Kootenay area of the 1890s, was real. Her students were intrigued, and they went home with heads full of Gertie's adventures. Hearing these stories at home, the kids' parents now bought the story, hook, line and sinker. Over the coming weeks Carolyn frequently had to explain that Gunpowder Gertie was the product of her imagination and had, in fact, never existed.

But all this got her thinking. She put together a package of her forged newspaper articles, a short summary that she had written of Gertie's life as well as a cover letter explaining that Gertie was fictional. Then she sent it off to *The Express*, a weekly newspaper in Nelson, BC, suggesting that it might make a good April Fool's story. But at some point between arriving at *The Express* and making to the editor's desk, the topsheet explaining that it was all an elaborate fiction had been lost. Once he read the story, the editor assumed it was all true and made ready to run the story. At this point, however, more knowledgeable heads prevailed, and someone pointed out that they knew for a fact that Gertie was a fictional character. *The Express* eluded Gertie's clutches.

Back in Crescent Valley though, the publisher of another local paper, the *Kootenay Review*, was a parent from the school that Carolyn taught at. He thought the story would make a great April Fool's joke—and it would be even more convincing if they ran it in May instead of April—and so was born the persistent legend of Gunpowder Gertie.

In the same way that Gertie had jumped into a life of piracy based on nothing more than a toy boat and the recollections of her grandfather, so too did anyone who heard her story leap to the conclusion that it was all true. No one checked up, no one researched, no one corroborated, no one, in fact, did anything but believe. It's typical of the relationship most of us have with pirate lore—we would rather believe than actually know.

When Carolyn called the producers at *This Day in History* to clarify things, someone said that with her skill at spinning a tale she should think about becoming a storyteller. And the more she thought about it, the more it made sense. She could take the story of Gertie on tour, to festivals, libraries and classrooms; she could celebrate her own interest in pirates and also spark interest in BC's history. Using her childhood treasure chest as a prop, Carolyn hit the storytelling circuit, taking Gertie's adventures to a wider audience.

And what of Gertie? In addition to being listed as a real person by most websites that mention her, she has also taken on life in other media. A short 10-minute video "biography" of Gertie was produced at some point, further fuelling the confusion. The Nelson Fall Parade has been known to feature a float in the shape of the *Tyrant Queen*. And Gertie's creator continues to tell her story at festivals in Yukon, Vancouver and other places both near and far.

The story of Gunpowder Gertie shows how easily fact and fiction can become confused when the word "pirates" is involved. What starts as a loose thread can quickly find itself spun into a yarn, and before you know it, an entire fabric has appeared, but one woven from thin air—emperors have gotten new clothes this way. If this sort of thing can happen in the 1990s, and still be believed more than a decade later, what does that say about the accuracy of stories that successive storytellers have been embellishing for two or three hundred years?

That said, it isn't hard to see why Gertie appeals to us so strongly—her story is that of an underdog who prevails. When she takes revenge on the society that has trodden her down, we can all share in her triumph. As she steams along on her adventures each of us can feel the thrill of dreams fulfilled. And finally, all of us can take heart in the unofficial family motto espoused by Gertie's grandfather:

Illegitimus non carborundum

"Don't let the bastards grind you down."

CHAPTER FOURTEEN

Oak Island: The Money Pit

...facts are stubborn things.

−J.B. McCully,
early treasure hunter on Oak Island

FOR MOST PEOPLE, WHOLEHEARTEDLY BELIEVING IN PIRATE legends has little impact on their day-to-day lives. For instance, believing that Gunpowder Gertie was real will not necessarily lead you to steal a steamboat and embark on a career of river piracy. But for more than 200 years, a little island in Mahone Bay, Nova Scotia, led successive generations of treasure hunters to spend fortunes and lose their lives in a, so far, futile hunt for buried millions. The name of this little speck in the ocean? Oak Island.

Oak Island is rumoured to be the burial site of something of great value. Since whatever that "something" is has never been found, no one can say precisely what it is, but the most common assumption is that it is a treasure of colossal value. Some say the island is the final resting place of Captain Kidd's hoard. Others have pointed out that Blackbeard once boasted of having buried his treasure where "none but Satan and myself can find it" (and by this, he clearly must have meant Nova Scotia).

The first part of the story is supposed to have started in the summer of 1795, when Daniel McGinnis, John Smith and Anthony Vaughn began digging in a small clearing on uninhabited Oak Island. McGinnis had found a depression in the earth under the branches of a large oak tree, and visions of buried treasure danced through his head. Soon the diggers encountered a layer of flagstones, which they removed, and then continued digging to a depth of 10 feet, where they found a layer of rotten logs that appeared to have been placed there deliberately. They kept digging and found additional layers of logs at 20 and 30 feet. Since then, on and off for more than 200 years, there have been people digging for treasure on Oak Island.

The second part of the story starts on October 16, 1862. On that day the *Liverpool Transcript* published the first recorded mention of these events nearly 70 years after they are supposed to have occurred. This and a subsequent article were both written by men who openly admitted they were part of consortiums trying to recover the treasure. Treasure hunting in those days could be big business; scam artists would sell "shares" in treasure-hunting ventures that never came to fruition. Indeed, as early as 1861, the *Transcript* had published an article called "The Oak Island Folly" that recounted a huge gathering of onlookers on a day when the treasure was supposed to be raised:

> *It was thought that about a fortnight ago they had struck upon the treasure; a day was set on which the copper-bound casks were to be raised from their long resting place—expectation grew high—shares sold at an enormous premium— hundreds of people flocked from all directions, and while each one was straining his eyes to get the first glimpse of the gold the middle hole "caved in," and disappointment was soon pictured on the countenance of each one present.*

Whether or not the early Oak Island treasure hunters were deliberately selling shares in bad faith is not known. But what is known is that the earliest accounts of the site's discovery were written by men who had every reason for wanting local readers to believe that pirate treasure was buried on the little island. If they were legitimately expecting to find it, the money from the shares would have allowed them to continue the work of digging out the pit. If they were scam artists, the money people paid them was just so much gravy in their pockets. Either way they needed trusting investors to pony up.

According to early accounts, the first Oak Island organization had been called the Onslow Group. It had consisted of McGinnis, Smith and Vaughn, backed by businessmen from Onslow and nearby Truro. They dug to a depth of 90 feet before the hole filled up with water. At that point work on the site ceased until the Truro Group began excavations in 1849 and 1861. It was stakeholders from the Truro Group who had written the articles that for the first time set down the supposed facts of the site's discovery. It was also during this time that the so-called Money Pit claimed its first victim: A labourer was scalded to death when a boiler ruptured. Years later another man died when a rope slipped out of its pulley and he fell into the depths of the pit.

As the 19th century continued, more groups took up the cause, most of them truly believing a treasure was at the bottom—but their beliefs were founded on quicksand. As the years went by, the so-called facts of the story became muddied and began to sound more like a boy's adventure story than anything rooted in truth:

• Although long dead, McGinnis and Vaughn began to be referred to as "boys," when documents actually place them in their mid to late 30s in 1795.

• Although it was uninhabited in 1795, the island had actually been parceled off into lots as early as 1762, and people may have lived there after 1768.

• McGinnis was frequently said to have discovered the island when rowing about looking for adventure, when in reality both he and Smith had owned lots on Oak Island for quite some time before the discovery of the money pit.

• It was claimed that the Onslow Group had found layers of logs every 10 feet up to a depth of 100 feet, when early accounts only refer to "marks" at 10-foot intervals after the layer of logs at 30 feet.

These were just some of the details that got lost in the mishmash of conjecture that was starting to pass for fact. It was further claimed that a mysterious slab of stone had been discovered 90 feet down. The stone bore mysterious "marks" that had been translated as "forty feet down, 2 million pounds are buried." Oddly enough, no one seems to have thought of taking a photograph of the stone, or a rubbing, before it conveniently disappeared sometime around 1919. The only known copy of the symbols dates from the first half of the 1900s and is highly suspect.

Indeed, by the first half of the 20th century, the legend was bigger and more unruly than ever—and so were the drilling efforts. By now so much earth had been removed that the location of the original money pit was completely unknown. Furthermore, many other shafts were sunk in an effort to drain the water that began pouring into holes deeper than 90 feet.

The source of the flood water remains mired in controversy to this day. Although it should come as no surprise to anyone that there is water 90 feet underground (on an island surrounded by the sea, no less), somewhere, someone had introduced the notion that the flooding was due to an extensive series of booby-trap tunnels that had been cunningly dug to flood the money pit should anyone get too close to the treasure. By the 1930s all sorts of other shafts started to appear as treasure hunters tried to prevent the water from pouring in.

The drills and dollar figures were also becoming more impressive.

Frederick Blair's family had been involved in the search since 1863, and he had formed the Oak Island Treasure Company in 1893. Forty years later, in 1933, he teamed up with an independently wealthy backer named Gilbert Hedden. Between 1934 and 1937 Hedden spent $51,400 shoring up the collapsing walls of one of the main shafts and continuing it to a depth of 160 feet—he found no treasure. Blair and Hedden had something of a falling out after this, but in the coming years the two of them continued to convince new backers to put up money.

The next partner to come on board was Erwin H. Hamilton, a professor of mechanical engineering from New York University. He spent $58,000 between 1935 and 1940, sinking 58 holes *horizontally* that branched out from Hedden's main shaft. The idea was to find the original money pit shaft and, hopefully, the treasure. He found something he thought was the old money pit—but not the treasure.

Treasure hunters came and went over the next decade, but in 1950 Frederick Blair hired Mel Chappell, then aged 63, to oversee the search. Chappell's father had been a treasure hunter during the 1890s and was as convinced as anyone that fabulous wealth was only a few thousand shovelfuls and many millions of gallons of water away.

When Blair died at the age of 83, he still hadn't seen any sign of the treasure he had spent his life searching for. Chappell took up the reins where Blair had left off, bringing in new capital and fresh blood.

Next came George Greene, a Texan with a cigar in his mouth. Among other things, Greene had once claimed to have found Noah's Ark, but now he represented a group of oilmen from Corpus Christi, who were determined to put their oil drilling expertise to use in discovering the treasure of Oak Island. Greene sank several 4-inch holes to depths of more than 180 feet before giving up. Chappell started looking around yet again for a new source of money.

In 1959 came the most unlikely treasure hunters yet—the Restall family. Bob and Mildred Restall had met in England in 1931. She was training to be a ballerina and he was a daring motorcyclist from Toronto, who performed in the circus. They married and went on tour together, Mildred joining the motorcycle act they now called the "Globe of Death." The two of them would each ride a motorcycle around the inside of a steel-mesh sphere, narrowly missing each other. They did this for 20 years before returning to Canada and attempting to lead normal lives. But in 1959, Bob heard about Oak Island and caught the treasure-hunting bug. Bob and Mildred, along with their two sons, Bobbie, 18, and Ricky, 8, set up a crude homestead on the island and started to dig.

The conditions were primitive—they lived in two huts, each one 16 feet square. There was no running water, no telephone and for the first three years there was no electricity. Also, the family's total life-savings was $8500, meaning that Bob couldn't afford the expensive drills and water pumps that earlier explorers had used. So every day, Bob and Bobbie would descend into one or the other of the numerous pits and hack away with picks and shovels. It went along like this until August 17, 1965. On that day, Bob, Bobbie and two other men were all overcome by some sort of gas in one of the shafts, lost consciousness and drowned in the water at the bottom.

The Restalls' search rights passed on to a man named Bob Dunfield. Starting in 1965 Dunfield spent $131,000 digging for treasure. First he built a little causeway from the mainland out to the island. Across the causeway he transported a 70-ton crane. With this monstrous piece of machinery he proceeded to clear out a pit that was *140 feet deep* and *100 feet across*. Then he filled the pit back in so that he could set up a mechanism to drill out deep core samples. He put two years of his life into the search, destroyed part of the island in the process and then got out. Still no treasure.

Even after six deaths and hundreds of thousands of dollars, there were always new people willing to believe that untold millions were under another few inches of water. By this time it was "common knowledge" that Oak Island's flooding pits were the result of a massive series of interconnected tunnels and shafts, many of which had been sunk to depths of more than 180 feet, sometimes through solid bedrock. According to believers, this ingenious system of purported booby traps had been constructed perhaps as long as 300 years ago, by pirates or other treasure hiders, who made it with nothing more than hand tools. They didn't have the benefit of steam power or pumps and also managed to leave almost no traces of this massive undertaking on the island itself, aside from a sunken depression under an oak tree. Such people dismiss the idea that natural water seepage could be responsible for the flooding of the pits.

In the early 1970s, people had been hunting for treasure on Oak Island for more than 180 years, and the site was becoming contaminated by old tools and dig shafts that had nothing to do with treasure and everything to do with treasure hunting. But still a new group of investors came forward: The Triton Alliance. Along with a man named Dan Blankenship, Triton would shape the next 35 years' worth of digs on the island. Triton had deep pockets and paid $15,000 for a feasibility study alone, shelling out a further $1,250,000 and still not finding any treasure. For his part, Blankenship sank a narrow shaft called Borehole 10x. Out of this came flakes of ancient manmade metal that have reportedly been dated to pre-1750 by no less an authority on metallurgy than Stelco Ltd. Blankenship also sent a camera down Borehole 10x and (along with others) claims to have seen a severed human hand, a submersed corpse and something that may have been a treasure chest, all in a flooded rock chamber more than 230 feet below the earth's surface. Still no treasure.

Other items found on the island include ancient coconut fibres, bits of wire and hand-worked metal from deep underground and a mysterious triangle of moss-covered stones arranged to point in the direction of the original money pit. There is more too, but like all evidence, any of it can be explained away by skeptics or used by believers to bolster their case.

Mel Chappell died in 1980, at the age of 93, having never found a single doubloon of the treasure he was searching for. To this day, Dan Blankenship and Triton continue to pursue separate efforts on Oak Island. Still no treasure.

And what pirates may we find here? Possibly the only pirates in the piece are the early groups of treasure hunters who sold shares in what amounted to nothing more than a hole in the ground. From there, local beliefs that pirates had once buried treasure nearby did the rest. Blackbeard and Captain Kidd were long dead, but they cast shadows long enough to fire the imaginations of Nova Scotians into the 1800s and beyond. Two hundred years, millions of the dollars and six lost lives later, the money pit is still gobbling up peoples' lives—and their life-savings.

Still no treasure.

Seven Things, or People, Thought to be Buried on Oak Island

- The Holy Grail

- Documents preserved in mercury, proving that Sir Francis Bacon was the author of Shakespeare's plays

- A "remolecularizer" buried by aliens

- The French Crown Jewels

- The Lost Treasure of the Knights Templar

- Secrets of the Lost Continent of Atlantis

- Jimmy Hoffa

CHAPTER FIFTEEN

The 20th Century and Beyond

What's past is prologue.

–William Shakespeare

As the 21st century gets under way, the only Canadian pirates you're likely to hear about are illegal downloaders of music and illicit reproducers of DVDs. The old fashioned "boat and sword" variety of buccaneers has been replaced by a new breed of digital thieves who use disc burners and shared files to plunder the intellectual property of others. That isn't to say that gun- and sword-toting pirates don't still put in an appearance every now and then. Throughout southern seas there are still documented cases of pirates who stage murderous assaults for little more than a few hundred dollars— it's just that their connection to Canada is tenuous at best. Indeed, since 1900, piracy has more often *happened to* Canadians than been practised by them.

Bob Medd is a Canadian who is lucky to be alive after a murderous attack on him in the Pacific Ocean in August 2001. He was sailing his 34-foot boat, *The Learning Curve* (*TLC* for short), in Mexico's

Gulf of California. Medd had retired at 55 and was fulfilling a lifelong dream—sailing solo in warm waters. Since leaving his home port on Vancouver's Sydney Island, he'd made his way down North America's west coast. Along the way he'd gotten used to buying fish from local vendors, who would usually come alongside in small boats, either selling their wares or asking for a drink of water.

One night Medd saw four men approaching in a little boat. He went below to get them some water and when he turned around, saw that one of them had come on board and followed him into the cabin. The man held a bread knife in one hand and had picked up Medd's wallet from where it sat nearby.

"Dinero, dinero!" the man said, demanding money. When Medd replied that he had only $200 in his wallet, the man slashed him across the arm. In the struggle that followed a second pirate came aboard and smashed Medd across the back of the head, most likely with a rock. With *TLC*'s owner unconscious, the men took everything they could find, and then slit Medd's throat. Medd survived, and when he came to, his boat had run aground somewhere on the coast. For the next two days he wandered the Desierto de Vizaino, a desolate ribbon of sand that runs for 65 miles down the coast. Finally he was rescued by some friendly fishermen, and with the help of his family got back to Canada.

Medd lost everything; he had no insurance for the boat and all of his money and valuables had been taken by the thieves. He had no house on the mainland since the *TLC* had been his home. He also had to undergo several costly operations to repair severed tendons and other muscle damage he had sustained in the attack. The doctors told him that if he hadn't been sporting a heavy beard at the time of the attack, the murderous knife slash across his neck would have killed him. With the help of his family, Medd overcame his problems and even came out of retirement to start earning again. He had lost everything, but he was glad to be alive.

And there are others. In February 1998, New Brunswick pleasure sailor Peter Mais was shot in front of his wife and children as their sailboat lay at anchor in Mochima National Park, Venezuela. Three men had fired at him from a small boat that had pulled up close by. When help appeared, the little vessel took off and didn't return. Peter's wounds were only superficial, but he and his wife Maggie were far more cautious sailors after that.

In 1995 British-born Nova Scotian Edward Chadband was anchored off the northeast coast of Colombia. At around noon one day, three local men approached him in a small boat and demanded money and gasoline. They sat in their boat looking at Chadband, one brandished a machete while the two others held clubs. Chadband's response was to strip naked and pee over the edge of his boat into the water. When this failed to frighten them away, he pulled out his flare gun, loaded it in front of them and finally pulled out a machete of his own that was much larger than theirs. This impressive display of phallic symbols seems to have worked, and the three men paddled off, none the richer, and probably now firmly in the grip of machete envy.

All things considered, pleasure cruisers in remote southern waters should take care. Piracy is rare these days, but it does happen, and any shipboard survival kit should include a well-reviewed plan for dealing with pirates. Since cannons are really no longer an option (especially on hobbycraft), the best bet is to do thorough research and avoid waters with a reputation for danger.

By far, the Canadians who suffer the most from modern-day piracy are fishermen. Illegal fishing in Canadian waters has a long and dishonourable pedigree. In the 1880s, the Great Lakes were the scene of strained relations as U.S. fishing ships blithely sailed into Canadian waters and began hauling in huge catches. To make things worse, even back then Canada had prudently set quotas on how many fish individual ships were allowed to catch. The U.S. had no such restrictions, and so not only were the American interlopers invading our waters, they were heedlessly hauling in catches as large as they pleased, with no thought towards preserving the industry for future fishermen.

Flash forward one hundred years: The battle has long since left the Great Lakes area and has now taken up residence on the east coast. In the 1990s, European cod pirates were in the news as fishermen from the Spain, Portugal and the UK took up fishing in Canadian waters, since theirs didn't have any fish left. In the early years of the 21 century, now having depleted Canadian cod stocks, these scaly buccaneers have taken their plundering closer to home, starting to overfish in the Barents Sea. In February 2007, Greenpeace released a report suggesting that ports in Holland and Spain were heavily involved in "illegal cod laundering."

Canadians are also guilty of overfishing their own waters. The Canadian government regulates how many pounds of a particular kind of fish can be caught in a particular area by a particular fisherman. These limits are called Individual Quotas (IQ), and every professional fisherman has his own IQ. Be that as it may, every year a handful of Canadian fishermen are fined for exceeding their own IQ, proving that it *is* possible to be too smart for your own good.

Pirates are supposed to be larger-than-life characters, and the Canadian of the species does not disappoint. In the course of this book we've met roguish gentlemen, hardened salts, murderous cutthroats, intrepid damsels not the least in distress, downtrodden women very much in distress, abusive husbands, scurvy dogs and possibly delusional treasure hunters. All of them, whether their stories are grand, mundane, inspiring or tragic, are at the centre of tales that to us, seem dramatic and exciting. But as we've seen, the passage of time often makes past events more palatable than they actually were. As the old saying goes, "It reads better than it lives."

Pirates are also good at getting us to flip our priorities and take leave of our senses: They count among their numbers murderers, rapists and thieves, committing crimes that are anything but victimless. But now, as always, our interest and in many cases our sympathies lie with the pirates; their victims get very little ink. Of course, often the victims are either dead or bankrupt or otherwise indisposed and have very little recourse in standing up for themselves. But in a strange twist of fate, at the time of this writing, two ships commanded by a Canadian and named after prominent Canadians have been dubbed "pirates" because they are standing up for animals who otherwise cannot defend themselves, namely whales.

The Sea Shepherd Conservation Society (SSCS) was founded in 1977 by Canadian Paul Watson after he dropped out of Greenpeace. The SSCS takes a far more militantly activist stance than Greenpeace (Watson allegedly called them "the Avon Ladies of the environmental movement"). To this end, the SSCS maintains a small fleet of ships specifically for disrupting whaling expeditions. The two largest ships are the 677-ton, 180-foot *Farley Mowat*, named after the famous Canadian writer and said to be armed with a water cannon and a hydraulic ramming blade with the strength of a bulldozer; the other is the 1017-ton *Robert Hunter*, named for the late Bob Hunter, journalist, broadcaster and co-founder of Greenpeace. Since 1979, SSCS ships have claimed responsibility for ramming at least six whaling vessels, as well as playing an active part in either sinking or disabling 10 others.

Despite a 1986 international moratorium on the hunting of whales, Iceland and Norway both continue to hunt them commercially, and Japan kills hundreds each year as part of a "scientific" whaling program. But on February 28, 2007, the Antarctic Japanese whaling fleet announced that it was returning early after a fire on its main ship killed a crew member. The expedition was 352 whales short of the 860 it had hoped to kill. During their six-week expedition, the Japanese fleet was continually hampered, and at times physically attacked by the *Mowat* and the *Hunter*.

At the beginning of February, the *Mowat* had been "deregistered" by Britain. Canada and Belize had revoked her registration six months previously. Furthermore, the UK authorities announced that the *Hunter* would also be deregistered within 30 days. According to Watson, Japan had pressured the countries into revoking their accreditation and, lacking proper registration, the SSCS's ships would become pirate vessels.

Undaunted, both ships followed the Japanese whalers on their expedition. The fleet consisted of the lead ship, *Nisshin Maru*, and five support vessels. The SSCS used various tactics to disrupt the hunt.

- Crew members threw smoke bombs on to the decks of the ships.

- They tried to jam the whalers' propellers by throwing ropes into the water.

- They threw butyric acid (a foul-smelling corrosive) on to the deck of one of the ships. The SSCS website erroneously listed butyric acid as being smelly but harmless, when in fact it can be very harmful if inhaled or absorbed through the skin. One Japanese sailor was injured when the acid splashed into his eye, and another was cut when the container hit him in the face. The SSCS website said the substance was acid, but Paul Watson said it was more or less rancid butter.

- Zodiac inflatable dinghies were launched from both the *Mowat* and the *Hunter*. The crews of these little craft pulled up alongside the drainage outlets of the *Nisshin Maru* and used nail guns to attach plates to the hull. The Japanese ship now had no way to expel blood and other whale-related waste fluids.

At one point, two of the SSCS crew were lost in heavy snow and fog. The Japanese vessels helped in the search for them, but once the crewmen were found, the SSCS again renewed their attacks. Finally though, just before Valentine's Day, both the *Mowat* and the *Hunter* were running out of fuel and headed for Australia. According to Watson, they were nearly 1240 miles away when a fire on the *Nisshin Maru* broke out. Indeed, the Japanese have never suggested that the fire, which killed one crewman, was directly caused by the SSCS, and Watson says that the *Nisshin Maru* caught fire once before in 1998 when it was on its way to another hunt. Nevertheless, Japanese spokesmen have been quick to dub Watson a terrorist, and many voices from within the international community have spoken out against him.

Paul Watson is a polarizing figure, and his actions, as well as those of the SSCS, are condemned by all governments and bodies. The International Whaling Commission has revoked the SSCS's status as a nongovernmental organization. Greenpeace strongly disagrees with SSCS's strongarm tactics. Troublingly, SSCS vessels are known to keep guns on board. In spite of the fact that no one has ever been proven to have died as a direct result of the SSCS's actions, many are disturbed by the inherent violence of their methods.

Here then is the central paradox of pirates past versus pirates present: When they sailed the seas 300 years ago murdering people left, right and centre, pursuing bloody gain at the expense of others, we celebrate them as jolly, if deadly, stereotypes. But when they sail the waters of today, even in pursuit of something so high minded as saving the whales, the minute they start smashing their ships into officially sanctioned vessels, pirates become "polarizing figures," "condemned by all government bodies"—in short, frightening, off-putting and disturbing—but still undeniably fascinating.

Pirate Lingo and Nautical Terms

In recent years, September 19 has been celebrated around the world as "International Talk Like a Pirate Day." Indeed, on this day, a global chorus of "Arr's," "Ahoy's" and "Avast's" can be heard to issue forth from all corners of the globe. Why do people do this? Is it because by momentarily speaking like a pirate we *become* a pirate? Try it sometime. Just stand up and say aloud "Shiver me timbers!" Not only will you feel a warm glow of rascally good feeling, but for an all too brief instant, the seven seas will have become your own personal playground: your trunk overfloweth with gold, your parrot screecheth "Pieces of Eight," and all is well with the world.

But did pirates really talk like this?

The truth of the matter is that we will never know how pirates spoke, but we can make some educated guesses. The first thing to remember is that pirates were, first and foremost, sailors. If we think of them as speaking in a sort of loopy pirate lingo, it is because this is the language of boats and the sea. Any sailor between the 17th and 19th centuries would have sounded to us like a pirate. And, whether, Canadian, British or American, most English-speaking sailors of the would have shared the colourful language that, right or wrongly, we think of as pirate-speak.

Ahoy: It first appeared in print in 1751, but sailors had been saying it for years as either a greeting (similar to "Hello") or a cry to get someone's attention (instead of "Hey!"). It seems to have stemmed partly from the exclamation "Hoy," which was first used as a way to call pigs, and later came into use when calling to humans as well. Alexander Graham Bell famously suggested "Ahoy" as the greeting for people to utter when they picked up his new invention, the telephone. Needless to say, it didn't take.

Arr: No one knows when this expression first came into use. It may very well be an artifact of 20th-century pop culture. Its general meaning is taken to be an expression of surprise, similar to "Oh!" If it actually does have any credence as real exclamation, it may stem from a bastardization of "Aye" for "Yes." Beware then, that when you say "Arr!" you may actually be saying "Yes," and therefore agreeing to some sort of piratical undertaking.

Athwart: At right angles to.

Avast: This expression is first recorded in print in 1681, meaning, "Stop!" or "Hold on!" It can also mean "Shut up!" or in more nautical terms, "Stow it!" There are many theories about its origin: It may come from the Dutch expression *houd vast*, for "hold fast," which in English is a shipboard expression for "hold that rope still" (i.e., stop pulling it). However, French, Italian and Spanish all share the term *basta*, which means "enough" (as in "Enough already!"). The Dutch option seems the more likely since we get many other nautical expressions from Dutch, including *schooner, sloop* and *yacht.*

Aye: No great mystery here. This is an expression of agreement or affirmation: "Yes." It was used on land long before it became doubled into the familiar "Aye aye, Sir" of sea-going lore.

Belay: In a purely nautical sense this means to secure a rope by winding it around a cleat or pin. But in swashbuckler films it is not unusual to hear a captain snap, "Belay that order!" meaning, "Stop right away!" Also, in sea stories and adventure novels, sailors defending their ship will sometimes seize a belaying pin to repel the boarders. Belaying pins were wooden pegs that could be moved around to different positions for the purpose of tying off ropes. They were comparable in size to a bowling pin and would have made a good instrument of blunt force in hand-to-hand combat.

Black spot: This is a device that seems to have been invented by Robert Louis Stevenson in *Treasure Island*. It consists of a black card, or piece of paper, given to a pirate by other pirates, signifying that its recipient is going to be killed for some wrong or transgression. Other writers have taken the idea and run with it to such an extent that it is now considered part of traditional pirate lore. Sometimes the black spot is a splotch of tar or pitch left on the victim's door, whereas other times it is a piece of white paper with a black spot on it.

Bow: The front, or "fore," end of a ship or, as some landlubbers say, "the pointy end of the boat."

Brig: A brig is a two-masted ship with the sails on both masts square rigged; that is, at right angles to the long axis of the ship. Seen from above a brig, it would look like this: ‡

Broadside: The simultaneous firing of all the cannons along one side of a gun ship. On a vessel with 32 guns, this would mean 16 cannons firing *at once*. Broadsides were incredibly loud and incredibly destructive. One tactic involved sailing up parallel to another ship and unleashing a broadside into the full length of the opposing vessel. This was risky of course, since your opponent might be planning exactly the same thing.

Carronade: Full-size shipboard guns might be 10 or 12 feet long, but carronades were miniature cannons designed to shoot full-size cannonballs over a shorter distance and at a lesser velocity than full-size guns. The slower-moving shot would result in many more flying splinters and therefore greater injury to the enemy's crew.

Cutter: A small boat carried aboard a larger vessel, either for going ashore or boarding other ships. Cutters might be powered by oars alone, or they might also have a mast and sails. The rowing arrangement of cutters was "double banked," meaning that for each pair of oars, two men would sit beside one another, each one pulling a single oar. Cutters had narrower sterns than longboats (see below).

Dance the hempen jig: This expression is a grim example of gallows humour, meaning "to hang" or "to be hanged." A jig of course was a traditional highland dance involving a lot of fancy footwork, much of it blindingly fast, sometimes making it seem as though the dancer is dancing on air. And a hangman's rope (along with most other rope) was made of hemp—not the smoking kind, but the rope-making kind.

Doubloons: As well as pieces of eight (see below), no chest of pirate treasure would be complete without doubloons. Doubloons were gold Spanish coins, and a handful was worth a small fortune to a pirate. "Doubloons" comes from the Spanish word *doblón*, meaning "double," but what exactly was being doubled remains unclear. It may have been because the first coins to be called *doubloons* were worth two *ducats*, or it could have been referring to the double portrait of Isabella and Ferdinand that graced them. Or it may have come from a later version of the coin, which was worth two *escudos* (yet a different kind of Spanish coin).

Fore: The front half of a ship.

Fore and Aft: Front and back. This was also a particular way of rigging a ship's sails in which the sails were set more or less along the length of the ship. Schooners had "fore and aft" rigs.

Four Pounder: A cannon firing a cannonball that weighs four pounds.

Gig: A small oared boat that might have several pairs of oars. Gigs were single-banked, meaning that a single rower pulled two oars, one in each hand.

Grog: Today, this is a chummy way of referring to any sort of alcoholic beverage, but not so long ago it meant cheap booze, and before that it specifically meant rum diluted with water. The legend of how grog got its name takes a bit of explaining, so you may want to fix yourself a drink and then come back. Ready? Here goes—to start with, there are two things you need to know.

1. *Grogram* was a kind of stiff fabric made from rough-spun, coarsely woven threads. Because it was tough and durable, it made excellent garments for seafaring men who were themselves tough and durable.

2. Sir Edward Vernon was a famous English sea captain who was tough and durable, and furthermore, wore a long coat made of—you guessed it—grogram.

Captain Vernon was frustrated by constant drunkenness among his crew and possibly also by the fact that they called him "Old Grog" because of his tough and durable coat. In 1745 Vernon ordered that each man's daily half-pint ration of rum was to be diluted with water, and in addition, would now be consumed in two portions *six hours* apart. His men, accustomed to corroding their throats with straight rum a half-pint at a time, didn't like this one bit. For one thing, it made it much harder to get drunk, and for another…well, it mainly just made it much harder to get drunk. Unimpressed with their watered-down refreshment, they started callng the drink "grog," in reference to the captain who had forced it on them.

Alas, the story just doesn't hold water—the word "grog" had been popping up in print for more than 20 years before Captain Vernon issued his famous order. It had first appeared in *The Family Instructor,* written by Daniel Defoe in 1718. It almost certainly comes from the West Indies and, before that, possibly Africa. It seems to refer to either a sweetened or fermented drink, and appears to have nothing to do with tough, durable fabric (though one might argue that any story containing the word "grogram" is worth telling).

Head: The bathroom on a boat or ship.

Ho: Before it was a rap lyric, this was an expression of joy or surprise, or of drawing attention to something sighted far off, as in "Land ho!"

Jolly Boat: Despite sounding suspiciously like the title of cheery children's book, this was a mispronunciation of the Dutch word *jolle*, which meant a small vessel with oars or sails kept in the stern of a larger ship—or as it is known in English, a *yawl*.

Jolly Roger: A long-standing nickname for a traditional pirate skull and crossbones flag. It may have come from the French *jolie rouge* (pretty red), after a kind of flag flown by French buccaneers, or from the 17th-century English expression "roger," for "rogue or devil." Or it might come from an oft heard Tamil phrase "Ali Raja," meaning "king of the sea." The theory here goes that English mariners would first have pronounced it properly, "Ali Raja," then "Ally Roger," then "Olly Roger," and finally "Jolly Roger."

Keelhaul: Sailors being punished in this manner would have weights tied to their feet, then they would be attached to a rope that ran across the width of the ship *under* the hull (and so under the water). Then they would be hauled back and forth across the keel while the ship was in motion. In theory, the weight attached to the victim's feet would keep him low enough in the water to avoid hitting the keel itself. But in some versions of the story, the whole point was to actually drag the "keelhaulee" across the barnacle-encrusted hull of the ship, slicing his skin on the sharp shells of the barnacles—if he hadn't already drowned, that is.

Letters of Marque: Documents issued by governments authorizing private shipowners (or "privateers") to attack and capture the vessels of enemy nations. In effect, letters of marque were a licence to pirate.

Longboat: A boat with several sets of oars, double-banked, meaning that two men would sit beside one another, each pulling one oar. Longboats had wider sterns than cutters (see above).

Matey: In a strictly nautical sense, this meant the first mate on a ship, but the phrase quickly came to mean brother in arms, buddy, chum, compatriot, and so on. It was also probably used sarcastically to address people who were not buddies, chums and so on.

Pieces of eight: The basic unit of currency in Spain during the age of piracy was the *réale*. In the same way that a dime is worth 10 cents, a piece of eight was worth eight *réales* and was also called a Spanish dollar. Minted from silver,

by today's values, a piece of eight was worth about $30 to
$35CDN. Since money was valued by the weight of its pre-
cious metal content and not by the face value, it was common practice to cut these coins into smaller bits shaped like
pie wedges, each one being worth approximately one *réale*.
The phrase seems to have started off referring to the entire
coin, but was then also used to describe its wedge-shaped
offspring. This is also why a quarter dollar is known as "two
bits," since it took two wedge-shaped bits to make up one-
quarter of the coin's full worth.

Port: If you're standing on the deck of a ship and facing
forwards, "port" is "left." It used to be called "larboard," but
somebody finally realized that this was confusing because
"right" is "starboard," and in high winds and crashing seas
orders could easily get confused.

Privateer: Vessels licensed by the government of one
country to capture the vessels of another country, sell their
cargoes and keep the profits. The word "privateer" could
apply to either the vessel itself or any of the men who crewed
her. Privateers were bound by law to carry letters of marque,
the government documents that more or less licensed them
to pirate.

Schooner: A vessel with two or more masts, and with
her sails rigged "fore and aft"; that is, running the length of
the boat (as opposed to "square rigged"—see below.)

Scurvy Dog: Scurvy, of course, was the disease con-
tracted by mariners on long voyages when they did not con-
sume enough fresh fruits or vegetables. Its unpleasant
symptoms included bleeding, spongy gums and bleeding
under the skin. The name for the disease may come from
the old expression "scurf," which meant "scab," and there's
a good chance that sailors knew perfectly well they were
calling each other "scabby dogs."

Shallop: An open boat with oars or sails, or both.

Shiver me timbers: Along with "arr" and "matey," this
expression of surprise is never far from the lips of pirates in
fiction and film. It is easy to imagine that the timbers being

shivered are those of a boat that has just struck a rock, or perhaps even the timber in a pirate's wooden leg. But, although they make sense, neither of these explanations appear to be true.

"Timbers!" was an exclamation of surprise (like "Goodness" or "Heavens!") but with no specific meaning. It first appears in the popular song, *Poor Jack,* by the English lyricist and composer Charles Dibdin (1745–1814). In it Dibdin describes a long, rambling sermon by a ship's chaplain. As a metaphor for the chaplain's tangled sentences and fancy words, Dibdin uses the image of a coil of rope, knotted and twisted around itself:

> I heard our good chaplain palaver one day
> About souls, heaven, mercy, and such;
> And, my timbers! what lingo he'd coil and belay;
> Why, 'twas just all as one as High Dutch;

In 1834, sailor-turned-novelist Captain Frederick Marryat appears to have invented the phrase "Shiver my timbers" in his book *Jacob Faithful*—and so was born a popular saying that, to this day, stubbornly refuses to actually mean anything.

Six Pounder: A cannon firing a cannonball that weighs six pounds.

Sloop: A single-masted ship.

Square rigged: A way of rigging a ship's sails so that they sit at right angles to the long axis of the ship. Seen from above, a square-rigged ship would look like this: ‡ .

Starboard: When you're standing on the deck of a ship facing forward, "starboard" is "right."

Stern: The rear or "aft" end of a boat. As some landlubbers say, "The back end of the boat."

Twelve pounder: A cannon firing a cannonball that weighs 12 pounds.

Notes on Sources

Author Unknown. "No One Ever Punished for Burning of 'Robert Peel.'" *Oswego Palladium Times*, April 17, 1947.

Bonnycastle, Sir Richard H. *Canada As It Was, Is and May Be*. Vol. II. London: Colburn, 1852.

Breverton, Terry. *Black Bart Roberts: The Greatest Pirate of Them All*. Gretna, LA: Pelican Publishing, 2004.

Burl, Aubrey. *Black Barty: Bartholomew Roberts and His Pirate Crew. 1718–1723*. Gloucestershire: Sutton Publishing, 2006.

Conlin, Dan. "A Private War in the Caribbean: Nova Scotia Privateering, 1793–1805." *The Northern Mariner*, VI, No. 4 (October 1996).

Cordingly, Dave. *Under the Black Flag: The Romance and Reality of Life Among the Pirates*. New York, NY: Harcourt Brace & Company, 1997.

Crooker, William S. *Pirates of the North Atlantic*. Halifax, NS: Nimbus Publishing, 2004.

Eagan, Jim. Personal Communication. February 2007.

Farmer, J.S., and W.E. Henley. *Slang and Its Analogues*. New York, NY: Arno Press, 1970.

Fuller, L.N. "'Bill' Johnson, Admiral of the Easter Patriot Navy." *Watertown Daily Times*, April 10, 1923, Afternoon Edition.

Glasner, Joyce. *Pirates and Privateers: Swashbuckling Stories from the East Coast*. Calgary, AB: Altitude Publishing, 2005.

Graves, Donald E. *Guns Across the River: The Battle of the Windmill, 1838*. Prescott & Toronto, ON: Friends of the Windmill/Robin Brass Studio, 2001.

Guillet, Edwin C. *The Lives and Times of the Patriots: An Account of the Rebellion in Upper Canada, 1837–1838, and The Patriot Agitation in the United States, 1837–1842*. Toronto: Ontario Publishing, 1963.

Hendrickson, Robert. *The Facts on File Encyclopedia of Word and Phrase Origins.* New York, NY: Checkmark Books, 2000.

Horwood, Harold, and Ed Butts. *Bandits & Privateers: Canada in the Age of Gunpowder.* Toronto, ON: Doubleday Canada, 1987.

Horwood, Harold, and Ed Butts. *Pirates & Outlaws of Canada: 1610–1932.* Toronto, ON: Doubleday Canada, 1984.

Howell, Douglass E. "The *Saladin* Trial: A Last Hurrah for Admiralty Sessions." *The Northern Mariner,* V, No. 4 (October 1995).

Hympendahl, Klaus. *Pirates Aboard! 40 Cases of Piracy Today and What Bluewater Cruisers Can Do About It.* Dobbs Ferry, NY: Sheridan House, 2006.

Jordan, Edward. *An interesting trial of Edward Jordan and Margaret his wife who were tried at Halifax, N.S. Nov. 15th, 1809, for the horrid crime of piracy and murder, committed on board the schooner Three Sisters, Captain John Stairs, on their passage from Perce to Halifax: with a particular account of the execution of said Jordan.* Boston: No. 75, State Street, for sale there and at No. 52 Orange Street, [1809?]

Kert, Faye. *Prize and Prejudice: Privateering and Naval Prize in Atlantic Canada in the War of 1812.* St. John's, NF: International Maritime Economic History Association, 1997.

Kert, Faye. *Trimming Yankee Sails: Pirates and Privateers of New Brunswick.* Fredericton, NB: Goose Lane Editions and New Brunswick Military Heritage Project, 2005.

Lossing, Benson. *The Pictorial Field-Book of the War of 1812.* New York: Harper, 1869.

Marshall, A.G. "Likes History of Patriot War." (Letter to the editor). *Watertown Daily Times,* May 1, 1923, Afternoon Edition.

McCurdy, W.H. (compiled by). *Trial of Jones, Hazelton, Anderson and Trevaskiss, alias Johnson, for Piracy and Murder on Board Barque* Saladin. Halifax, NS: Petheric Press, 1967.

McTaggart, Carolyn. Personal Communication. February 2007.

O'Connor, D'Arcy. *The Secret Treasure of Oak Island: The Amazing True Story of a Centuries-Old Treasure Hunt.* Guilford, CT: Lyons Press, 2004.

Perkins, Simeon. *The Diary of Simeon Perkins.* Vols. 1–5. Toronto, ON: Champlain Society, 1948–1977.

Robertson, William Morrison Jr. *The Confederate Privateers.* New Haven, CT: Yale University Press, 1928.

Snider, C.H.J. *Under the Red Jack.* Toronto, ON: Musson, 1928.

Snow, Edward Rowe. *Pirates and Buccaneers of the Atlantic Coast.* Beverly, MS: Commonwealth Editions, 2004.

Stanley, George F.G. "William Johnston: Pirate or Patriot." *Historic Kingston,* No. 6, December 1957. Kingston, ON: Kingston Historical Society.

Stonehouse, Frederick. *Great Lakes Crime: Murder, Mayhem, Booze & Broads.* Gwinn, Michigan: Avery Color Studios, 2004.

Web Sources

Conlin, Dan. The Canadian Privateering Homepage. Retrieved March 10, 2007, from http://www.chebucto. ns.ca/~jacktar/privateering.html

Dobrota, Alex. "Farley Mowat, Pirate of the Antarctic." Retrieved March 10, 2007, from http://www.theglobeandmail.com/

Greenpeace. "Greenpeace Exposes Large-Scale Illegal Cod Laundering in the Netherlands." Press release dated February 7, 2007. Retrieved March 10, 2007, from http://www.commondreams.org/news2007/0207-07.htm

Joltes, Richard. "History, Hoax and Hype: The Oak Island Legend." Retrieved March 10, 2007, from http://www.criticalenquiry.org/oakisland/

McGuirk, Rod. "Activist a 'Pirate,' Not Eco-Terrorist." Retrieved March 10, 2007, from http://www.guardian. co.uk/worldlatest/story/0,,-6447342,00.html

Neighbour, Margaret. "Whaling Protesters are Pirates of the Antarctic as Ships Deregistered." Retrieved March 10, 2007, from http://www.scotsman.com/

Nickell, Joe. "The Secrets of Oak Island." Retrieved March 10, 2007, from http://www.csicop.org/si/2000-03/i-files. html

Pross, Catherine. "Barss, Joseph." Retrieved March 10, 2007, from http://www.biographi.ca

Vallar, Cindy. "Pirates and Privateers: The History of Maritime Piracy." Retrieved March 10, 2007, from http://www. cindyvallar.com/piratearticles.html

Geordie Telfer

GEORDIE TELFER IS A WRITER, actor, and artist in Toronto, Ontario. As a child, he practised flying by leaping onto a beanbag chair, and his dream job was to become Batman. Unfortunately, neither ambition turned out, but his passion for adventure remains. Geordie has been the assistant director for the Toronto Studio Players Theatre School, a freelance set carpenter, and a web and television writer. He worked extensively on deafplanet.com, the first TV show and website in American Sign Language, and has written several nature documentaries. Geordie has always been interested in the swashbuckling adventurers we call pirates, and this project is dear to his heart.